IT HAPPENED IN
CONNECTICUT

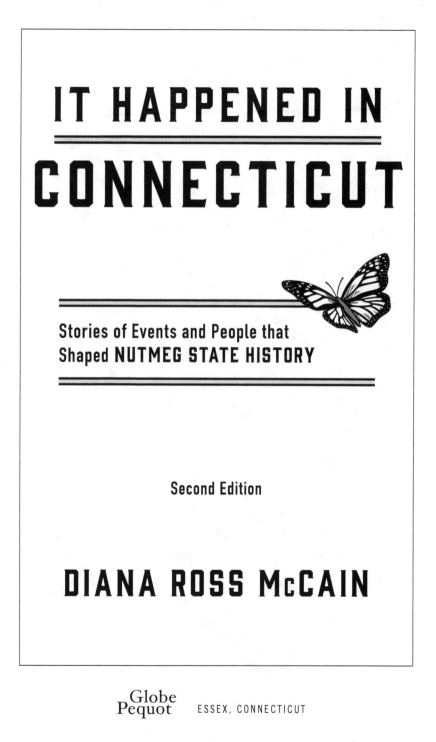

IT HAPPENED IN
CONNECTICUT

Stories of Events and People that
Shaped **NUTMEG STATE HISTORY**

Second Edition

DIANA ROSS McCAIN

Globe
Pequot   ESSEX, CONNECTICUT

Globe
Pequot

An imprint of Globe Pequot, the trade division of
The Rowman & Littlefield Publishing Group, Inc.
4501 Forbes Blvd., Ste. 200
Lanham, MD 20706
www.rowman.com

Distributed by NATIONAL BOOK NETWORK

British Library Cataloguing in Publication Information available

Library of Congress Cataloging-in-Publication Data
Names: McCain, Diana Ross, author.
Title: It happened in Connecticut : stories of events and people that
    shaped Nutmeg State history / Diana Ross McCain.
Other titles: Stories of events and people that shaped Nutmeg State history
Description: Second edition. | Essex, Connecticut : Globe Pequot, [2023] |
    Series: It happened in series | Includes bibliographical references and
    index.
Identifiers: LCCN 2022052421 (print) | LCCN 2022052422 (ebook) | ISBN
    9781493070381 (paper ; alk. paper) | ISBN 9781493070398 (electronic)
Subjects: LCSH: Connecticut—History, Local—Anecdotes. |
    Connecticut—Biography—Anecdotes. | Connecticut—Social life and
    customs—Anecdotes.
Classification: LCC F94.6 .M38 2023 (print) | LCC F94.6 (ebook) | DDC
    974.6—dc23/eng/20221104
LC record available at https://lccn.loc.gov/2022052421
LC ebook record available at https://lccn.loc.gov/2022052422

♾™ The paper used in this publication meets the minimum requirements of
American National Standard for Information Sciences—Permanence of Paper
for Printed Library Materials, ANSI/NISO Z39.48-1992.

For my sons, Jay and Ross
The best things that ever happened
to me in Connecticut

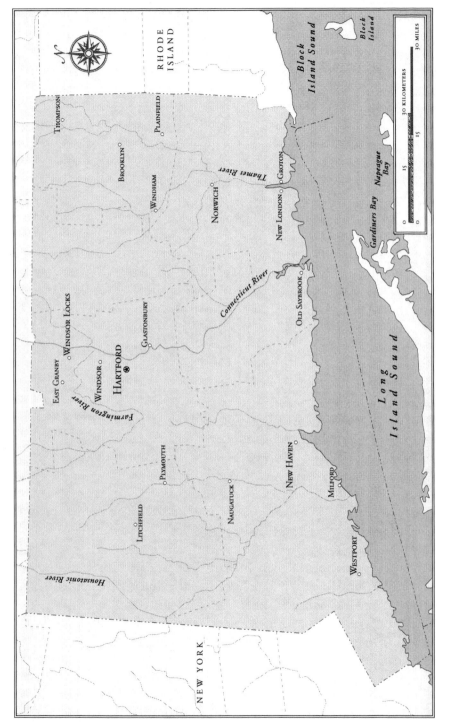

CONNECTICUT

CONTENTS

PREFACE

I have had a passion for history for as long as I can remember. I grew up in Ohio, which has a rich and proud past, but where a building that dates from the early 1800s is considered rare and ancient. When I moved to Connecticut in 1977, I looked forward to being able to explore earlier chapters in American history up close.

Connecticut did not disappoint. All around there are iconic town greens, steepled meetinghouses, clapboard homes—many of them two or three hundred years old, some even older. Here many Connecticut men and women played their roles in the saga that culminated in the establishment of an independent United States. Walls made of weathered and moss-covered stones serve as reminders of both the challenge confronting farmers who cultivated the state's rocky soil, and their resourcefulness in turning an irritant into an asset. Art and epitaphs on centuries-old tombstones speak with terse eloquence of the hopes, beliefs, and pursuits, as well as the trials, triumphs, and tragedies of thousands of individual lives that comprise the chapters of a community's heritage. Connecticut not only met my expectations; it exceeded them—and served up more than a few surprises. I was prepared to encounter famous figures such as Revolutionary War martyr/spy Nathan Hale in Connecticut's past. But who expects to find Mark Twain playing a featured role in Connecticut history? Or tycoon J. P. Morgan? Or vaude-ville legend Sophie "last of the red-hot mamas" Tucker?

It came as a disconcerting surprise to discover that Black people had been held in slavery for the first two centuries following Connecticut's settlement, or that men and women had been executed here on witchcraft charges. I hadn't known about Connecticut's emergence during the 1800s as a giant of industry, which it remained well into the twenti-eth century. Factories manufacturing everything from guns to silk to kitchen appliances for a global market had attracted immigrants from Sweden, Italy, Ireland, Russia, and every-where in between. Decade after decade they had come, by the tens of thousands, until by the middle of the twentieth century Connecticut was one of the most ethnically diverse states in the nation.

Just as saltboxes and stone walls bear witness to the first two centuries of Connecticut's history, the transforming devel-opments of the 1800s and 1900s are represented by everything from factories to cathedrals, from synagogues to social clubs to the State Capitol itself—another surprise. Built in 1878, when Connecticut was on the rise as an industrial powerhouse, the Capitol features so much intricately assembled stained glass, elaborately carved stone and wood, and ornate, vividly colored stenciling that it looks more like an ancient, exotic palace than the seat of government of the "Land of Steady Habits."

Learning about Connecticut history has been only half the fun. The other half has come from sharing fascinating stories from the state's past through articles, columns, and books such as this one. I hope these twenty-seven chap-ters will serve as glimpses of the intriguing, diverse, and immensely entertaining array of people and events that com-prise nearly 400 years of Connecticut history.

1647–1663

The First Witchcraft Executions in North America

Say "witchcraft trials," and most Americans immediately will think of the 1692 Salem, Massachusetts, hysteria, dramatized by Arthur Miller's play *The Crucible*, during which twenty men and women were executed for allegedly practicing sorcery. But Connecticut got nearly a half-century jump on Salem; the first person known to have been executed in North America on charges of practicing witchcraft was hanged in 1647 in Hartford.

Witchcraft today may be the stuff of Halloween fun, Hollywood blockbuster fantasy, and phenomenally popular book series, but it was a serious business in seventeenth-century Connecticut—deadly serious. New Englanders, like Europeans, sincerely believed in the existence of witches, who wielded supernatural powers acquired through a deal with the Devil himself.

To New Englanders in the 1600s, everything that happened was part of the eternal struggle between God and Satan and their followers; nothing occurred by chance. Thus when unexplained misfortune befell a person—a child became sick, livestock fell ill, a barrel of beer turned bad—the first reaction was to look for someone with a grudge.

As to what should be done with witches, the Bible, on which Connecticut's Puritan settlers based all aspects of their lives, was clear: "Thou shalt not suffer a witch to live." When the Connecticut Colony drew up its first code of laws in 1642, being a witch was included among the crimes punishable by death.

The victim of the landmark 1647 execution was Alice Young of Windsor. Nothing is known about the specific accusations or evidence brought against this woman who was the first of at least eleven individuals put to death on charges of witchcraft in Connecticut before the end of the seventeenth century.

The very next year Mary Johnson of Wethersfield confessed that "shee is guilty of familliarity with the Deuill," and went to the gallows on witchcraft charges. In 1651 Goodwife Bassette of Stratford allegedly admitted to being a witch and was executed. In a culture that believed in demonically acquired magic, some people may very well have thought they were witches. Some may have been pressured onto an admission. Most accused witches, however, denied the charges. Some were acquitted—and some were not.

In 1651 John and Joan Carrington of Wethersfield were convicted of "not hauing the feare of God before thine eyes thou hast Interteined ffamilliarity with Sathan the great Enemy of God and mankinde and by his helpe hast done works above the Course of nature." The sentence "thou deseruest by dye" was pronounced, and husband and wife met their deaths at the end of a hangman's noose.

Two years later in Fairfield, Goodwife Knapp was tried for witchcraft. One of the pieces of evidence presented was the alleged presence on her body of "witch's teats"—small tags of flesh from which the Devil purportedly suckled his followers. Found guilty, Knapp resisted intense pressure by a parade of visitors to confess to being a witch. She maintained her innocence to the day she was hanged.

In 1654 Lydia Gilbert of Windsor was brought up on charges of witchcraft for allegedly causing the death of a man three years earlier in an accident for which another person had already been held responsible. On October 3, 1651, Henry Stiles, a boarder in the house of Thomas and Lydia Gilbert, was killed during a militia exercise when the gun of the man marching behind him, Thomas Allyn, went off accidentally. Allyn admitted that he had been careless with his firearm, was found guilty of "homicide by misadventure," and was fined twenty pounds. Case closed—but not for good.

Three years later, the Connecticut court, for reasons never explained, refunded Thomas Allyn's fine and charged Lydia Gilbert with using witchcraft to orchestrate Stiles's death at Allyn's hand. Found guilty, Gilbert was presumably hanged.

Even when the charges were horrific, there seems to have been no rush to judgment. Nicholas and Margaret Jennings of Saybrook were accused of witchcraft in 1661. Among their alleged crimes was that, with Satan's help, they had caused the deaths of several people, among them a child. Although the jury felt strongly that they were guilty, some members didn't feel the evidence was solid enough for a conviction

3

that would result in the couple's death. The Jenningses were freed, but they lost custody of their two sons. They eventually sought sanctuary in Rhode Island.

Witchcraft fever flared up in Hartford and surrounding towns in 1662. In that year alone, nine people were tried for witchcraft—and four were found guilty and sent to the gallows.

That eruption was touched off by the accusations of an eight-year-old girl. Elizabeth Kelly of Hartford suddenly was taken ill with pains in her abdomen and shortness of breath, which she claimed were caused by an invisible assault by Goodwife Judith Ayers. The child, crying out that Ayers would kill her, begged her father to chop off Ayers's head with an ax. Although this sounds similar to the later events in Salem, in which girls experienced painful fits that they accused others of inflicting by diabolical, invisible means, there was no chance Elizabeth Kelly was pretending. After four days of torment, the little girl died.

The child's deathbed accusation weighed heavily against Ayers. At her father's insistence, the first-ever autopsy in Connecticut was performed on Elizabeth Kelly in an effort to learn the truth. The procedure was done grave-side five days after the girl died. The primitive state of medical science at the time and the apparently limited anatomical knowledge of the physician who conducted the autopsy led to the judgment that the cause of Elizabeth Kelly's death had been "preternatural"—that is, inexplicable by ordinary means. Goodwife Ayers and her husband watched the case against her grow ever more damning. They were jailed, but friends broke them out, and the couple fled to Rhode Island. Like the Jenningses, they had to leave their two sons behind.

The next victim was Mary Sanford of Hartford. Although both she and her husband were tried for witchcraft, only Mary was convicted and sent to the gallows.

Another young Hartford woman, Anne Cole, claimed she was being physically tortured by witches. Anne named names, among them Rebecca Greensmith, described by a local minister as a "lewd, ignorant and considerably aged woman."

Both Rebecca Greensmith and Nathaniel Greensmith, her third husband, were hauled into court on witchcraft charges late in 1662.

Nathaniel Greensmith maintained his innocence, but Rebecca confessed to being a witch. She admitted that she engaged in sex with Satan himself. One night, testified Mrs. Greensmith, she met under a tree on the South Green in Hartford with what she implied was a group of witches, including "James Walkley, Peter Grant's wife, Goodwife Ayres, and Henry Palmer's wife, of Wethersfield, and goody Seager." They danced and drank wine.

Mrs. Greensmith accused her husband of witchcraft as well. Nathaniel Greensmith denied his wife's stories of his rendezvous with mysterious animals in the woods, of his demonstrations of superhuman strength, but in vain. Both husband and wife were found guilty. They met their end on the gallows on January 18, 1663, along with another woman convicted of witchcraft, Mary Barnes of Farmington.

As in the case of the Jenningses in Saybrook, not everyone accused by Anne Cole or Rebecca Greensmith was found guilty of witchcraft. In 1663 Elizabeth Seager of Hartford beat the witchcraft rap twice, despite testimony that she was observed to fly, was spotted dancing around a cauldron with two suspicious creatures, and spoke in strange, mysterious ways. Tried yet a third time for witchcraft in 1665, Seager was found guilty, but her conviction was reversed, and she was set free. She fled Connecticut.

Other accused witches found it prudent to follow Seager's example and get out of Connecticut while they still had the chance. Judith Varlett, mentioned by Rebecca Greensmith, spent time in jail but was never charged, and she left Connecticut after being released. Henry Palmer of Wethersfield and his wife, Katharine, one of the women named by Rebecca Greensmith, also found themselves under official investigation for witchcraft.

They managed to avoid prosecution, and eventually the family moved to the relative safety of Rhode Island. James Walkley of Hartford, yet another person accused by Rebecca Greensmith, was investigated for witchcraft; he jumped bail and fled to Rhode Island.

During the remaining decades of the century, more than a dozen additional people were charged with witchcraft in Connecticut, but none were executed. The hysteria that infected Salem, Massachusetts, in 1692 was reflected in a spike of eight witchcraft accusations made the same year in southern Connecticut, five of them in Fairfield.

Two of the Fairfield accused, Mercy Disborough and Elizabeth Clawson, underwent, at their request, the controversial "water test," in which the accused was bound hand and foot and thrown into a pond. It was a potentially no-win situation for the alleged witch. If the suspect floated, this was interpreted as the pure water rejecting the corrupted body of a witch. If the suspect sank, it was considered evidence of innocence. This latter finding, however, was helpful only if the accused, trussed up at the bottom of a pond, was rescued before she drowned.

Despite their claims of innocence, both women floated. But when a special court of ministers took up the case, they dismissed the water test as "unlawful and sinfull" and therefore useless as evidence.

Elizabeth Clawson was acquitted of the witchcraft charges, one of the strongest arguments in her favor being a statement signed by more than seventy-five individuals who knew her and had the courage to attest that she had been "sivil and orderly towards others." Disborough was not so fortunate as to have that volume of support and was found guilty and condemned to death. Her sentence was delayed until the next meeting of the General Court, and she was ultimately granted a permanent reprieve.

There are almost as many theories about what was truly behind the seventeenth-century New England witchcraft accusations and trials as there were victims. Some possible explanations put forth include fear and suspicion of strange, eccentric people, usually but not always women, living on the fringes of mainstream society; the anxiety of the harsh life on the frontier, exacerbated by epidemics and food shortages; hallucinations caused by eating rye bread containing the fungus ergot; long-festering resentments between different factions in a community; political unrest that spread great fear among the populace; and people settling old scores or trying to move up on the backs of others.

Whatever the cause or causes, Connecticut soon abandoned the belief that witchcraft was a legal offense. The law making witchcraft a crime was removed from the books by 1750.

1660–1689

Refugees from Royal Revenge

Seventeenth-century Connecticut was the playing field for a deadly game of cat and mouse in which agents of the king of England pursued three of the men responsible for beheading the monarch's father. For decades the regicides—"killers of the king"—eluded the royal hunt, thanks to the help of prominent leaders and ordinary citizens from Hartford to Guilford to New Haven to Milford.

William Goffe, Edward Whalley, and John Dixwell were among the fifty-nine signers of the death warrant that sent England's King Charles I to the chopping block in 1649 on charges of high treason. For the next decade England was a commonwealth, whose government was dominated by Puritans, of whom the Lord Protector Oliver Cromwell was the most powerful.

But the commonwealth didn't long survive Cromwell's death in 1658. In the spring of 1660, Charles I's son, who had escaped to continental Europe following his father's execution, agreed to return to rule England as King Charles II.

The king and Parliament pardoned those who had committed offenses during the long period of bloody turmoil through which England had just passed—except the regicides. Thirteen of the signers of Charles I's death warrant who fell into his son's hands were executed by hanging, drawing, and quartering, the grisly punishment reserved for traitors. This gruesome procedure began with hanging the condemned man but cutting him down while he was still alive, then castrating and disemboweling him and burning his organs in front of him, and finally beheading him and hacking his corpse into four pieces. The head and body quarters were distributed to different areas of England to be put on public display as a warning to any who might contemplate treason.

Whalley, Goffe, and Dixwell saw the bloody writing on the wall for the regicides in time to escape. All three would eventually seek refuge among fellow Puritans in New England.

On May 14, 1660, Whalley and Goffe sailed from England under assumed names. They arrived in Boston on July 27 to a warm welcome that cooled toward year's end when news reached Massachusetts that they were wanted regicides. In February 1661 they left Boston and traveled for nine days across more than 140 miles of wilderness to reach New Haven, then the nucleus of a colony of the same name. The New Haven Colony was an entirely separate entity from the Connecticut Colony, which was centered around the Connecticut River towns of Hartford, Windsor, and Wethersfield. Both colonies were subject to the English Crown.

The New Haven Colony was the purist of the Puritan settlements in New England. Whalley and Goffe were housed as honored guests in the home of the colony's founding father, the Reverend John Davenport. In a ruse designed to deceive any pursuers, Whalley and Goffe set off for Milford, nine miles west of New Haven, to create the impression that they were heading for the Dutch settlement of New Amsterdam, today's New York City. That night, however, they secretly returned to Davenport's house, where they hid for a month. By the end of April, King Charles II had issued a proclamation for Whalley and Goffe's capture, put a bounty on their heads, and sent a warrant for their arrest for "the execrable murther of our Royal Father" to Boston.

The governor of the Massachusetts Bay Colony commissioned two men to find the regicides and take them into custody. But warnings and clandestine assistance from supporters enabled Whalley and Goffe to stay ahead of the manhunt—sometimes barely one step ahead.

On April 30, two days after the warrant for their arrest reached New Haven, Whalley and Goffe moved from Davenport's house to another New Haven dwelling. The Massachusetts commissioners arrived at the Guilford home of William Leete, acting governor of the New Haven Colony, on May 11. Before the day was over, a messenger had covered the eighteen miles from Guilford to New Haven to alert Whalley and Goffe of their danger. The regicides took refuge in yet another hiding place, a mill about two miles west of New Haven.

Acting Governor Leete stalled the commissioners in order to give Whalley and Goffe as much time as possible to escape. Leete either dragged his feet in filling the commissioners' requests for assistance or claimed he lacked the authority to act. By the time the commissioners finally reached New Haven on May 13, Goffe and Whalley had fled to the forest for safety.

Leete and the New Haven Colony magistrates proceeded to play a perilous game. They made a show of "cooperating" with the commissioners while continuing to hinder their search with bureaucratic roadblocks and red tape. The frustrated commissioners accused Leete and his fellow officials of wanting the regicides to get away and cautioned them that "his sacred Majesty would resent such horrid and detestable concealments and abettings of such traitors and regicides." The commissioners reminded the colonists that the penalty for concealing or helping a traitor was the same as that for the traitor himself: hanging, drawing, and quartering. They threatened the continued survival of the entire New Haven Colony. At the same time, they also offered substantial rewards for information about the regicides' location.

But all the commissioners' bluster and bribes failed to ferret out Whalley and Goffe's whereabouts. After two fruitless days of searching, they moved on to look for the regicides in New Amsterdam. The day after the commissioners' departure, Whalley and Goffe moved to yet another new hiding place: a cave atop a ridge on the border of the modern towns of Hamden and New Haven, which is today called West Rock.

In the middle of June, Whalley and Goffe heard rumors that Davenport was still suspected of concealing them. Determined that he and others who had sheltered them should not suffer for helping them, the regicides decided to surrender to the authorities. They went to New Haven to turn themselves in, but changed their minds and before officials, moving deliberately at a turtle's pace, could get around to detaining them, fled back to their West Rock cave.

By the end of August, the Massachusetts commissioners had given up their quest and sailed from New Amsterdam back to Boston. With the heat off, at least temporarily, Whalley and Goffe felt they could risk leaving their cave for the more comfortable refuge of a private home in Milford. There they stayed for more than two years, rarely daring to step outside the house.

In England, rumors circulated that Whalley and Goffe were in Belgium or Switzerland or Holland, or even that they had been killed. But King Charles remained unconvinced. When in 1664 he dispatched representatives and a force of 450 soldiers to assess the status of the New England colonies and conduct negotiations with the Dutch at New Amsterdam, he also instructed them to continue the search for the regicides.

Upon receiving this alarming news, the regicides left Milford and returned to the West Rock cave. On October 13, 1664, they struck out, traveling only at night, until they reached the town of Hadley, more than seventy-five miles to the north on the Massachusetts frontier. There they hid for the next decade in the house of the Reverend John Russell.

In February 1665 Whalley and Goffe were reunited in Hadley with fellow regicide John Dixwell. After escaping England, Dixwell had gone first to Germany before making his way to New England.

Edward Whalley died in Hadley sometime between August 1674 and August 1676. By the summer of 1676, William Goffe had relocated to Hartford. There he remained in hiding until his death, which is believed to have occurred about three years later.

How long John Dixwell stayed in Hadley, and where he went when he left, is not known. He turned up in New Haven by 1673 under the alias "James Davids." Although Dixwell kept mostly to himself and maintained a low profile, there was speculation about his identity and personal history. Only a few trusted friends knew the truth.

In 1673 the sixty-six-year-old Dixwell married for the first time—only to have his wife die just a month later. In 1677, now seventy, Dixwell wed Bathsheba How, who at thirty-one was less than half his age. The couple had three children.

John Dixwell, alias James Davids, died in New Haven on March 18, 1689, at the age of eighty-one. He was buried in the cemetery on the New Haven Green under a simple gravestone carved with the terse inscription "J.D. Esqr. Deceased March ye 18th in ye 82d year of his age 1688/9."

A possible explanation for the cryptic inscription is the fact that a regicide could not rest easily even in death. Several regicides who had died in England before King Charles II was restored to the throne had been "posthumously executed"—their corpses dug up and subjected to hanging, drawing, and quartering.

In April 1689 news reached New Haven that King James II, who had become ruler of England upon the death in 1685 of his brother Charles II, had been forced from his throne the previous December. James had been replaced by his daughter and son-in-law, who would reign as William and Mary. The new royal couple had no interest in continuing the vendetta against the regicides, most of whom were dead anyway. Although John Dixwell never knew it, the game had ended with the Puritan mouse outlasting the royal cats Charles II and James II—if only by three months.

Dixwell's humble gravestone still stands on the New Haven Green, and the rough cave in which Whalley and Goffe hid can be visited in West Rock Ridge State Park. Both recall a time when residents of Connecticut put themselves in danger to protect men driven into exile for defying a royal despot.

1665

Hostile Takeover, Colonial Style

History books call it a "union" or an "absorption." But "hostile takeover" would more accurately describe what happened to the New Haven Colony in 1665. The New Haven Colony, which had been founded and had functioned as an entirely independent government for more than two decades, was swallowed whole against its will by the Connecticut Colony, its larger, richer, more politically savvy neighbor to the north.

The stage for the takeover scenario had been set in the 1630s. In 1635 and 1636, separate groups of Puritans from Massachusetts had settled the towns of Windsor, Hartford, and Wethersfield on the Connecticut River. In 1639 those three settlements had united under a framework of government known as the Fundamental Orders, and the Colony of Connecticut officially came into existence.

To the southwest of the river towns, yet another band of Puritans from Massachusetts had settled in 1638 at what today is New Haven. In 1643 New Haven and several other nearby settlements, including Guilford, joined to form the New Haven Colony.

Both colonies expanded geographically over the course of the next quarter century. By 1660 the Connecticut Colony included the land on both sides of the Connecticut River from Windsor to Saybrook on Long Island Sound, as well as a tract that ran all the way to Stonington on the east and Norwich to the north. Its territory also extended as far west as Farmington and even included towns such as Norwalk, Fairfield, and Stratford on the southwestern coast of Long Island Sound.

The New Haven Colony grew less aggressively than Connecticut. By 1660 it extended as far north as Hamden, as far east as Guilford, and as far west as Milford, and even included Stamford and Greenwich on the coast. That its expansion didn't match that of Connecticut might have been due in part to the fact that its laws and practices were far stricter. The New Haven Colony's government, based solely on the Bible, was a true melding of church and state. Anything not provided for in the Bible, such as trial by jury, wasn't included in the New Haven Colony's framework of government, which was headed by a seven-man panel. In order to vote, a man had to be a member of the church, in contrast to the Connecticut Colony, which had no such requirement.

As different as the two colonies were in governmental structure and geographic size, they had one very important thing in common. Neither Connecticut nor New Haven had clear-cut, unequivocal legal permission from the English government, which held title to most of New England, to have settled where they did or to establish governments. Both colonies had been settled at a time when governmental affairs in England were in turmoil, leaving officials in London little time or attention to devote to what was happening on the North American frontier. That welcome neglect continued while England was embroiled in civil war between 1642 and 1649 as well as during the subsequent decade, when England was governed as a commonwealth in which Puritans were a powerful force.

During that period of more than two decades, the Connecticut and New Haven colonies considered their lack of formal authorization from the Crown a technicality of little concern. But it was suddenly a very big problem for both in 1660, when King Charles II assumed the English throne, left vacant by his father's execution in 1649 authorized by a death warrant whose signers included many Puritans. Securing the Crown's seal of approval for their existence became an urgent priority for both colonies.

The Connecticut Colony was in a far better position to pursue official recognition than was the New Haven Colony. On March 14, 1661, Connecticut dispatched to the court in London its governor, John Winthrop Jr., whose namesake father had been one of the founders of the Massachusetts Bay Colony. The younger Winthrop was an intelligent, worldly, well-educated, well-connected man of many talents—including a genius for negotiation and diplomacy. The New Haven Colony, on the other hand, couldn't even afford to send a representative to England to plead its case.

On April 23, 1662, as a result of Winthrop's dealings, King Charles II granted the Connecticut Colony a royal charter of government that was almost too good to be true. The charter granted Connecticut the right to elect its own governor, deputy governor, and legislature, consisting of both an upper and lower house. The legislature was empowered to pass its own laws, restricted only by the vague requirement that they be "not Contrary to the Laws of this Realm of England." It was an extraordinary degree of self-government that amounted to near independence from English control.

The charter also included another provision that had been among the goals Winthrop sought when he arrived in London. That provision spelled out Connecticut's borders as precisely as possible in an era when most of North America was terra incognita: Connecticut was bound on the north by Massachusetts, on the east by the Pawcatuck River, and on the west by the "South Sea," or Pacific Ocean. (No one at that time had any idea just how wide North America was.) And the colony's southern border was "the Sea," meaning Long Island Sound. Therefore, according to the royal charter, the Connecticut Colony's territory included all of the New Haven Colony.

The new royal charter was read in Hartford on October 9, 1662. Later that month a delegation from the Connecticut Colony delivered the de facto death warrant to New Haven Colony officials.

New Haven Colony leaders had no intention of tamely submitting to Connecticut control, royal charter or no, but not all of the colony's residents agreed. The citizens of Stamford and Greenwich soon defected to Connecticut. Their willingness to break away might have been due in part to the rigidity of the New Haven Colony's government.

Despite these losses, New Haven Colony leaders continued their resistance to the takeover. Some found the prospect of becoming part of the Connecticut Colony, with its relatively lax religious and political structure, so distasteful that for a time they considered relocating to New Netherlands, the Dutch colony that included present-day New York City.

The unpleasant negotiations—if they could be called that—toward unification dragged on for more than a year. The Connecticut Colony dispatched representatives to New Haven to discuss the details of "settling the union and incorporation." New Haven charged Connecticut with "unjust pretences & Encroatchments."

The quarrel was threatening to become a regional crisis when a royal commission, consisting of 450 troops, arrived in April 1664 to assess the state of affairs in New England. Colonial leaders feared the two colonies' inability to come to an agreement that satisfied the conditions of the royal charter could give the king's representatives a convenient excuse to punish both colonies and might even endanger the legitimacy of other charters, such as that of Massachusetts.

New Haven was fighting a battle it could not hope to win. At the end of October 1664, the royal commissioners reinforced the terms of the charter, granting all of the New Haven Colony to Connecticut.

New Haven finally threw in the towel in December 1664. The "union" of the Connecticut and New Haven colonies was completed in April 1665.

That the union occurred, and endured, owed much to the foresight of William Leete of Guilford, who was governor of the New Haven Colony when the royal charter was granted to Connecticut. Leete initially opposed the union, but within a year of the charter's granting he started to take steps to ensure that what he saw as an unavoidable transition occurred "in a righteous & amicable way."

In October 1664 Leete agreed to serve in the upper house of the legislature that would be created to govern the merged

19

colonies. Gestures such as this by the New Haven Colony's governor toward peaceful compromise made absorption by Connecticut more tolerable for many New Haven Colony residents.

The union of New Haven and Connecticut was more firmly cemented when Leete, having been elected deputy governor of the Connecticut Colony, became governor upon John Winthrop's death in 1676. The following year he was returned to the governor's post by the voters and was reelected every year thereafter until his own death in 1683.

But not all New Haven Colony residents had been able to bring themselves to accept absorption by Connecticut. In 1666 a band of determined holdouts from Branford, Guilford, Milford, and New Haven left to establish a new settlement at what today is Newark, New Jersey.

1718–1790

Israel Putnam, Original American Folk Hero

Before there was Davy Crockett, before there was Daniel Boone, there was Israel Putnam of Connecticut. Putnam was a fearless frontier warrior, adventurer, and explorer who, even before the American Revolution, was "so well known throughout North-America that no words are necessary to inform the public any farther concerning him," as one Rhode Island newspaper wrote. And some of his most important and thrilling exploits were yet to come.

Born in Massachusetts in 1718, Putnam settled in 1740 in what today is the town of Brooklyn, in northeastern Connecticut, then largely wilderness. Two years later, in the winter of 1742–1743, Putnam performed the first of the phenomenal feats that would make him a legend in his own lifetime. He and his fellow farmers tracked a wolf that had been ravaging their flocks of sheep to its lair—a narrow, forty-foot-deep cavern.

Only Putnam, at the risk of his own life, had the guts and daring to go in after the animal. He wriggled his stocky body deep into the cave, shot the marauding wolf, and dragged it out by its ears. The cave, located in what today is Mashamoquet Brook State Park in Pomfret, can still be visited.

In 1755 Putnam joined the forces that Connecticut, as a colony of the British Crown, had raised to assist Great Britain in its war with France and each side's respective Native American allies in North America. In the Battle of Lake George in New York, he distinguished himself for his coolness under fire. Soon he became a leader of Rogers Rangers, a unit tasked with secret, dangerous reconnaissance missions.

Putnam's career—and life—nearly ended prematurely in 1758, when he was captured by a Native American ally of the French. Putnam had been bound to a tree, and the fire intended to incinerate him had been lit, when a French officer intervened and stamped out the flames. Putnam became a prisoner of the French, who transported him to Montreal and then Quebec. He was eventually ransomed from captivity and returned to Connecticut.

Putnam's reputation as a tough, smart warrior and leader who feared neither man nor beast, who had cheated death more than once, had spread to England itself. At forty years old, the bluff, hearty, salt-of-the-earth Connecticut farmer was an international celebrity.

Putnam was soon back in the military, rising to the rank of colonel by 1761. Spain had now sided with France in the ongoing international conflict with Great Britain, the North American part of which is known as the French and Indian War. Putnam commanded a Connecticut regiment that joined the naval expedition sent to attack Havana, on the Spanish-controlled island of Cuba. Vile weather and virulent disease turned the venture into a deadly disaster of epic proportions. Of the 107 members of Putnam's company, only 20 made it back to Connecticut alive.

The Cuban debacle didn't dampen Putnam's thirst for adventure. In 1764 he commanded Connecticut troops dispatched to Detroit, on what was then the western frontier. Their mission was to support British troops fighting a coalition of Native American tribes under the leadership of Pontiac, an Ottawa, that opposed British encroachment on their lands.

Putnam was back in Connecticut by the end of 1764. But he hardly had time to catch his breath after nine years of nearly continuous military service on far-flung battlefields before he became embroiled in a different kind of fight right at home. This battle was against Great Britain's attempts to exert greater control over its North American colonies through new taxes and legislation. It would be waged, at least initially, with words—sometimes inspiring, sometimes threatening.

In 1765 the British Parliament imposed a tax, payment of which was signified by a government stamp, on a variety of paper products used in the colonies, including newspapers and legal documents. Colonists from New Hampshire to Georgia reacted with outrage to this Stamp Act, which had been passed without their consent.

Putnam was one of the founders of Connecticut's branch of the Sons of Liberty, a radical group that opposed the Stamp Act and any other attempts to restrict colonists' rights. His celebrity and popularity gave credibility to the organization, for which he vigorously recruited members. Putnam also inspired thousands of Connecticut citizens to attend protest meetings against the Stamp Act. He even met personally with the governor of Connecticut to caution him against enforcing the Stamp Act.

In 1768 Putnam began running a tavern on the Brooklyn town green, to which he had moved from his original homestead two years earlier. Taverns were that era's community information centers. The latest developments were gleaned from travelers and newspapers, and important issues could be debated by local residents. It was a perfect arrangement for a power player like Putnam.

But yet another frontier beckoned to Putnam in 1772. The British government had given a shaky promise of a grant of land in the lower Mississippi valley to a group of colonial veterans of the French and Indian War as reward for their military service. Putnam led an expedition to explore the territory in question, sailing around Florida into the Gulf of Mexico. He stopped at Pensacola, Florida, and then proceeded on to New Orleans, ultimately traveling more than two hundred miles up the Mississippi River.

Putnam returned to Connecticut in 1773. In less than two decades, he had journeyed as far north as Quebec, as far northwest as Detroit, as far south as Cuba, and as far southwest as Vicksburg, Mississippi. It was a phenomenal travel record. He had seen more of the North American continent than just about any man of his era. In the decade since passage of the Stamp Act in 1765, the relationship between Great Britain and its colonies had steadily deteriorated. It seemed increasingly likely to result in bloody violence.

Like a good industrious Yankee farmer, Israel Putnam was at work by eight o'clock on the morning of April 20, 1775, plowing a field near the Brooklyn green in preparation for spring planting. Suddenly a rider appeared with news that the previous morning Massachusetts Minutemen and British redcoats had exchanged deadly musket fire in the towns of Lexington and Concord. Putnam left the plow and horse in the field where they stood and rode off to alert Connecticut Governor Jonathan Trumbull of the momentous development. The war for American independence had begun.

By the end of May, Putnam had been appointed a major general in the new Continental Army, as the patriot forces keeping the British bottled up in Boston had been named. On June 17, 1775, he found himself engaged in combat against British troops on whose side he had served just ten years earlier.

Putnam was one of the officers commanding a force of about 1,400 raw recruits charged with defending Bunker's and Breed's hills in Boston against an assault by nearly twice as many professional British soldiers. Three times the redcoats stormed the American fortifications, and three times they were driven back with terrible losses.

That the inexperienced defenders held their ground was credited in large part to the encouraging presence of that living legend, Israel Putnam. Some accounts say that "Old Put" steadied the men with the memorable order "Don't fire until you see the whites of their eyes!" When the patriots finally retreated from Bunker's and Breed's hills, it was only because they had run out of ammunition.

The British evacuated Boston in March 1776. Their next target would be New York City. General George Washington, the Continental Army's commander-in-chief, sent Putnam to oversee preliminary military preparations. During the major campaigns and battles that followed, it became evident that

Putnam lacked the ability to effectively command large numbers of troops in formal combat.

But "Old Put" still possessed his legendary courage, daring, and determination, as he demonstrated in February 1779. Putnam was commanding a brigade stationed in southwestern Connecticut when a British raiding party took him by surprise in Greenwich. He escaped capture by plunging his horse down a hillside so steep and rocky that his British pursuers weren't willing to follow.

Late in 1779 a paralyzing stroke accomplished what nothing else—not a ferocious wolf nor hostile British, French, or Native Americans—had been able to do: put an end to Putnam's heroic exploits. But "Old Put" wasn't done making history.

In 1788 Putnam's life story, written by fellow Continental Army officer and Connecticut native David Humphreys, was published in Hartford. The book was the first biography of an American written by an American. It went through thirteen editions, including ones issued by printers in New York and Philadelphia.

Israel Putnam died on May 29, 1790, and was buried in Brooklyn. In 1888 his remains were reinterred in the base of a twelve-foot-tall equestrian statue of the hero erected by the State of Connecticut near the Brooklyn town green. In the century following his death, pilgrims to Putnam's grave had chipped off so many pieces of his original tombstone for souvenirs that to preserve it it was removed and put on display in the Connecticut State Capitol in Hartford, where it can be seen today. The qualities that had made Putnam one of America's earliest folk heroes are summed up in a single line carved into that stone: "He dared to lead where any dared to follow."

1773–1827

Newgate's Caverns for Criminals

"This establishment ... is designed to be, from all its arrangements, an object of terror, and everything is accordingly contrived, to make the life endured in it as burdensome and miserable as possible." This was British traveler Edward Kendall's grim assessment in 1807 of Newgate Prison in East Granby, where for more than half a century men convicted in Connecticut of the most serious crimes were incarcerated.

Newgate had opened a century before Kendall's visit, not as a correctional facility, but as a copper mine. Despite decades of determined digging, it never proved to be a particularly profitable enterprise.

Then, in 1773, the Colony of Connecticut saw the failed mine as a promising "fixer-upper" in which the worst criminal offenders could be confined. A three-man legislative committee expressed confidence that with a modest amount of renovation to the property, "it would be next to impossible for any persons to escape." Cost-conscious Yankee leaders also were attracted by the possibility of having the convicts work the mine to help offset expenses.

The Colony of Connecticut spent $375 to purchase the mine and convert it for use as a prison. It was known from the beginning as Newgate Prison, after the infamous London jail of the same name.

Connecticut's Newgate could be described as Hell chilled over. Convicts entered by climbing down a ladder in a shaft more than twenty-five feet deep. Their accommodations were the tunnels that had been hacked out of the stone bowels of Connecticut by miners seeking valuable ore. The caverns were cramped, dark, often dank, and consistently cold, with the temperature hovering between 40 and 52 degrees year-round.

Between 1773 and 1827 more than 650 criminals did time in Newgate. It was an era when justice was swift and punishment harsh.

Men were sent to Newgate for more than a dozen different crimes, including horse stealing, burglary, forgery, highway robbery, rape, attempted rape, attempted murder, arson, counterfeiting, assault, manslaughter—and adultery and bigamy. Typical sentences could range from two years for burglary or forgery to six years for arson or counterfeiting to life in prison for attempted rape, attempted murder, or highway robbery.

The first prisoner sent to Newgate was John Hinson, who arrived on December 2, 1773, to serve a ten-year sentence for burglary. Despite colonial officials' boast that busting out of Newgate would be impossible, Hinson did exactly that just twenty days after he got there. Hinson is believed to have shinnied to freedom up a seventy-foot-long rope dropped down a well shaft by a confederate on the outside—a female friend, according to one version of the story. He was never apprehended.

The next five men incarcerated in Newgate also broke out before the end of April 1774—although it is possible that two of them actually died when the mine tunnel they were trying to enlarge into an escape route caved in on them. The next month construction was completed on a small wooden building over the main entrance shaft that was also intended to board two miners hired to help the prisoners work. The well through which John Hinson had escaped was blocked off with iron bars.

But these improvements failed to make Newgate escape-proof. Before the year was out, six more men, armed with tools they had taken by force from the two miners, overpowered the warden and fled. Most of the fugitives were returned to a prison that, thanks to the repeated escapes, had a new policy: leg shackles for prisoners. The felons were undeterred: two more escape attempts occurred in 1775.

The outbreak of the American Revolution in April 1775 created entirely new categories of offenders requiring incarceration: Tories—or Loyalists, as those who maintained their allegiance to King George III during the American Revolution preferred to be called. Newgate, its poor security record notwithstanding, received many of them. Late in 1775, General George Washington, the Continental Army's commander-in-chief, was in Cambridge, Massachusetts. On December 7, 1775, he sent to Newgate for safekeeping prisoners he described as "having been tried by a court martial and deemed to be such flagrant and atrocious villains, that they cannot by any means be set at large or confined in any place near this camp." Several dozen Tories were sentenced to Newgate because of their unpopular sentiment.

Despite repeated efforts to make the prison more secure, such as adding structures and increasing the number of guards, escape attempts continued to be a regular occurrence at Newgate. Early in 1776 eight prisoners set a considerable quantity of charcoal on fire, intending to generate heat intense enough to crack a boulder that blocked a drainage tunnel through which they hoped to flee to freedom.

Three of the would-be escapees (including one of those committed to Newgate by Washington a few weeks previously) died from inhaling the deadly fumes that filled the cavern. The rest survived, still prisoners.

On May 18, 1781, the door to the caverns was opened to allow a prisoner's wife to enter for a routine visit. Twenty-eight convicts, including several Tories, seized that brief window of opportunity to attack the prison's two dozen guards en masse. The prisoners managed to overpower the guards and force them into the cave. The altercation left one guard dead, six more wounded, and a number of prisoners injured. Most of the prisoners who managed to escape in that break-out were quickly recaptured.

In November 1782 the wooden building over the mine entrance went up in flames, ignited by prisoners as part of yet another escape attempt. Newgate was temporarily closed. It wasn't used to incarcerate wrongdoers again until 1790, when it became the official Connecticut state prison.

Improvements made at this time included construction of two subterranean "rooms" equipped with crude, built-in wooden bunks for the prisoners; a brick building over the mine's entrance to house guards and the warden and his family; a small prison "hospital"; a shop with eight forges (the state's new bright idea for helping offset expenses was to have the prisoners make nails); and other support buildings. These structures were enclosed by an eleven-foot-tall wooden fence, topped by five-inch iron spikes to discourage prisoners from trying to scale the walls to freedom.

Subsequent years would see replacement of the wooden fence with a twelve-foot-tall one made of stone, and construction of even more support buildings, including a kitchen, a chapel, and workshops in which the convicts could labor at other pursuits, such as making shoes or barrels. For the prisoners, though, the "new" Newgate was little better than the old one.

"The gloomy dungeons within its walls call to remembrance a Bastile, the prisons of the Inquisition, and other engines of oppression and tyranny," historian John Warner Barber wrote of the caverns in which prisoners were kept except when they were allowed on the surface to work. The British visitor Kendall observed that prisoners emerging from beneath the earth to start their day "were heavily ironed, and secured both by handcuffs and fetters; and being therefore unable to walk, could only make their way by a sort of jump or a hop.

On entering the smithery, some went to the sides of the forges, where collars, dependent by iron chains from the roof, were fastened round their necks, and others were chained in pairs to wheelbarrows."

Troublesome prisoners could be whipped—but no more than ten lashes. For those who didn't fall into line after that punishment, Newgate had its own version of the "hole"—a small room in which a man would be placed alone, chained to a rock and fed only bread and water.

Escape attempts were a regular occurrence at the reopened prison. Between 1790 and 1827 there were at least a dozen efforts to break out. Some escape attempts involved one man working alone; others involved a dozen or more. In 1822 the entire prison population of approximately one hundred men staged an unsuccessful escape attempt.

As early as 1816 discussion of replacing Newgate with a more humane facility began to circulate, prompted in part by emerging theories about rehabilitating lawbreakers rather than just warehousing them. In 1827 Newgate closed, and its inmates were transferred to a brand-new state prison in Wethersfield.

For one man the prospect of new, and presumably better, accommodations wasn't sufficient reason to stay. On the night before the prisoners were moved to Wethersfield, Abel Starkey tried to break out using the method that had worked for Newgate's first inmate and escapee, John Hinson—grappling his way up a rope to the surface and freedom. But the rope broke, and Starkey fell to his death.

The State of Connecticut sold the Newgate Prison property in 1830 to private individuals, who launched yet another effort to work the mines. This venture, and ones that followed it, proved no more successful than those of the 1700s.

Eventually, the prison buildings and underground facilities were allowed to crumble and fall into disrepair. Then, in a supreme bit of irony, the ruins of the prison that so many had tried so hard to escape became a privately operated tourist attraction during the latter half of the nineteenth century. Visitors took guided tours of the subterranean caverns that once housed hardened criminals.

In 1968 the State of Connecticut once again purchased the Newgate Prison property—this time to serve as a museum. The Old New-Gate Prison and Copper Mines, declared a National Historic Landmark in 1973, is open from May through October for the public to visit—and, unlike its original occupants—leave whenever they want.

1775–1776

Stealth *Turtle*

In October 1775 Benjamin Franklin stopped in Old Lyme, Connecticut, to see a demonstration of a new secret weapon for use in America's war for independence from Great Britain. On a remote site on the eastern bank of the Connecticut River near where it joins Long Island Sound, Franklin watched the world's first working manned submarine sink out of sight beneath the marshy surface and then reemerge some distance away.

The vessel was the invention of David Bushnell, who was born in nearby Westbrook, Connecticut, around 1740. Lack of money had prevented Bushnell from pursuing his dream of enrolling in Yale until 1771. Once there, he made up for lost time. While in college Bushnell conducted experiments demonstrating that a wooden container of gunpowder submerged in water would, when ignited, not fizzle out as had been thought but would instead explode with tremendous force.

As the American colonists' resistance to Great Britain's infringements on their rights seemed increasingly likely to end in war, Bushnell's discovery became of more than academic interest, for the British navy was the most powerful in the world. Bushnell developed a larger version of his experiment: a wooden cask that held 150 pounds of gunpowder and a timing device to ignite it. Bushnell believed that any ship could be sunk by detonating this "submarine mine" or "torpedo," as he variously called it, beneath its hull.

In the winter of 1774, Bushnell began fabricating a vessel to deliver his new mine to its target. The project took on greater urgency when fighting broke out between Great Britain and the colonies at the battles of Lexington and Concord in Massachusetts on April 19, 1775.

Secrecy being essential, Bushnell set up his weapons project on Ayers Point, a remote spot in Old Saybrook on the west bank of the Connecticut River. His younger brother, Ezra, assisted him with the project, which they told people was a fishing venture.

The result was a masterpiece of imagination, improvisation, and precision. The submarine was made of two large concave pieces of oak fitted together and held tight by iron hoops. A coat of tar made it watertight.

To the modern eye it looks something like an egg standing upright on its narrow end. Because the submarine resembled two turtle shells fastened together, Bushnell's contemporaries nicknamed it the *Turtle*.

Approximately seven feet high and three and a half feet in diameter, the *Turtle* could hold just a single crewman. This "operator," as Bushnell called him, entered the submarine through a round brass hatchway on the top that had tiny windows as well as openings to let air in when the *Turtle* was above the waterline.

The operator, who sat on a wooden plank, did literally everything. He powered the submarine by cranking a propeller on the side one way to move forward, and in the opposite direction to move backward. He did the same with a propeller atop the *Turtle* to move the vessel up or down. He steered with a wooden rudder. To submerge, he stepped on a plunger that allowed water to flood into the bottom of the vessel, causing it to sink as deep as twenty feet. To surface, he used a hand pump to expel that water.

When the *Turtle* was submerged, or when it operated with its hatchway above water at night, it was pitch black inside. With a bit of practice, the operator could become familiar enough with the location of the pedals, handles, and levers to work them in the dark. But he also needed to consult a simple compass to set and maintain the *Turtle*'s course as well as a specially developed device to monitor its depth. To see these instruments, illumination was essential. A candle, the eighteenth century's obvious answer, proved impractical, because the flame's consumption of oxygen cut into the thirty-minute supply of air the *Turtle* held while submerged.

The ingenious solution was foxfire, a fungus that feeds on rotting wood and gives off a greenish neonlike glow. Bushnell affixed small pieces of foxfire to the compass points and to the depth finder.

To deliver the mine, which was attached to the *Turtle*'s exterior by two large bolts, the operator would approach his target underwater. Once beneath the ship, he would use a hand crank to screw an auger, located on top of the *Turtle*, into the hull. He would then release both the auger and the mine, which were connected by a rope.

Detaching the mine also armed its timing device. The operator had twenty minutes to make his getaway before the mine exploded.

Bushnell had the perfect operator for the *Turtle*—his brother. Ezra Bushnell had helped fabricate the vessel, possessed the exceptional physical strength required to operate it, and had practiced countless hours in it.

On August 7, 1775, Dr. Benjamin Gale, one of the few trusted friends in whom Bushnell had confided about his project, penned an extensive description of the *Turtle* to Benjamin Franklin, then a delegate to the Continental Congress in Philadelphia. That letter prompted Franklin to stop on his way to Boston to see a demonstration of the promising new weapon.

The logical place for the *Turtle*'s maiden voyage was Boston. The redcoats had been holed up in the city since the battles of Lexington and Concord, and a large number of British ships were anchored in the harbor.

At the last minute, though, a simple surprise of nature thwarted the plan; foxfire stops glowing in very cold temperatures. The *Turtle* couldn't attack until the weather turned sufficiently warm for foxfire to glow. By the time that happened, patriot forces had forced the British to evacuate Boston.

The British next targeted New York, a city "so encircled with deep, navigable water, that whoever commands the Sea must command the town," in the words of one patriot general. By the end of July 1776, the British had assembled in and around New York harbor one of the largest naval forces in history—more than four hundred vessels.

Connecticut Governor Jonathan Trumbull arranged for the *Turtle* to be transported to New York. Again fickle nature foiled the plans. Ezra Bushnell contracted an illness that left him too weak to pilot the *Turtle*. David Bushnell recruited another operator, Sergeant Ezra Lee, and they and the *Turtle* returned to Connecticut for a crash course in operating the submarine.

By the time the *Turtle* finally went into combat on the night of September 6, 1776, the patriot situation had become desperate. On August 27 the British had crushed the Continental Army in a battle on Long Island. George Washington had saved his troops from annihilation by evacuating them to Manhattan Island by boat on a single, fog-shrouded night.

The *Turtle* targeted the enemy fleet's brain: the HMS *Eagle*, flagship of the British navy, with Admiral Sir Richard Howe on board. The largest vessel in the enemy's floating forces, armed with sixty-four cannon, the *Eagle* was anchored near the island on which the Statue of Liberty stands today.

Two rowboats towed the *Turtle* from a Manhattan dock as close to the *Eagle* as they dared. From there Lee piloted the *Turtle* on the surface for more than two hours until he was close enough to hear voices from the *Eagle*.

Lee submerged and maneuvered the *Turtle* underneath the *Eagle*. He tried to screw the auger into the ship's hull, but instead of burrowing into wood as expected, it struck something it couldn't penetrate. Before he could try another spot, Lee lost control of the *Turtle*, which bobbed to the surface. Fortunately, no one on board the *Eagle* noticed.

Extreme exhaustion and approaching dawn forced Lee to break off the mission. Heading back to Manhattan, a malfunctioning compass forced him to surface to keep the vessel on course. The *Turtle* was spotted by British soldiers, who set out in a boat to investigate the strange craft.

In order to move faster, Lee jettisoned the mine (thereby automatically arming it), which rose to the surface. At the appearance of this novelty, caution overcame curiosity among the approaching British. They backed off from the mine—which twenty minutes later exploded with such tremendous force that some people mistook it for an earthquake or a meteor strike.

The *Turtle* returned safely to Manhattan. David Bushnell concluded that the mission had failed for two reasons. Lee had had the misfortune to strike an iron plate in the *Eagle*'s keel with the *Turtle*'s auger. And Lee was neither strong enough nor sufficiently skilled in operating the *Turtle* to try a second spot.

The *Turtle* made two more attempts to sink British vessels in the Hudson River. Both were unsuccessful. The submarine was stowed on board an American ship anchored in the Hudson for temporary safekeeping. On October 9, 1776, a British bombardment sank the vessel containing the *Turtle*. Bushnell said he salvaged the *Turtle*, but nothing more was heard of it.

David Bushnell subsequently enlisted in the Continental Army and fought for American independence until war's end in 1783. He lived for several years with his brother Ezra's family on the Westbrook farm. Ezra died in 1787, and several months later David Bushnell simply disappeared.

No one in Connecticut had a clue what had become of David Bushnell until 1826, when his brother Ezra's descendants received word of his death in Georgia, where he had lived for nearly forty years under the alias of Dr. David Bush. He bequeathed them a substantial fortune, which he had accumulated by teaching, practicing medicine, and dealing in real estate.

The *Turtle* was perhaps too technologically advanced for its time. George Washington himself was of the opinion that too many factors had to fall into place perfectly for the *Turtle* to succeed against a foe as vigilant as the British navy. Nonetheless, Washington wrote in 1785, "I then thought, and still think, that it was an effort of genius."

Modern replicas of the *Turtle* are on permanent display at the Connecticut River Museum in Essex, Connecticut, and at the Submarine Force Library and Museum in Groton, Connecticut.

1776

Melted Majesty

Inflamed by a public reading of the newly adopted Declaration of Independence on July 9, 1776, a mob of soldiers, sailors, and civilians in New York City struck a symbolic blow at British tyranny by tearing down an enormous equestrian statue of King George III that stood at the southern tip of Manhattan Island. Within days, two thousand pounds of lead fragments from the toppled statue were headed for Connecticut to be converted into ammunition that patriot soldiers would use to make a literal impact on the bodies of British forces sent to crush the bid for American liberty.

The statue of "Our Most Gracious Sovereign" had been erected in 1770 on Bowling Green, a small, egg-shaped greenspace that still exists as a park. It depicted a larger-than-life George III, dressed as a Roman emperor and mounted on a warhorse. Coated in glittering gold leaf, it stood atop a fifteen-foot-tall marble pedestal. A ten-foot-tall iron fence surrounded Bowling Green.

The royal sculpture had been commissioned by the New York General Assembly in "Gratitude, and the Reverence due to his Sacred person and Character," for several developments, including Britain's recent victory in 1763 in the French and Indian War, and the repeal in 1766 of the Stamp Act that had outraged colonists screaming, "No taxation without representation!"

But just five years after the statue was erected, relations between the colonies and Great Britain had soured. The tensions erupted into actual warfare on April 19, 1775, in the battles of Lexington and Concord, Massachusetts.

On July 4, 1776, the Declaration of Independence was approved by the Continental Congress in Philadelphia. On July 9, Commander-in-Chief George Washington ordered that the Declaration be read aloud to Continental Army troops gathered in lower Manhattan preparing to defend New York against a massive British armada sent to put down the rebellion. The document's stirring claims of liberty, and its laundry list of offenses by George III, inspired the toppling of the Bowling Green statue, which protestors hacked into pieces.

The statue was made of lead, an essential component of musket balls. After more than a year of fighting, lead was exceedingly scarce in America. The very next day, plans were underway for making practical use of the precious metal. Continental Army Lieutenant Isaac Bangs, stationed in the city, recorded in his journal on July 10 that "The Lead, we hear, is to be run up into Musquet Balls for the use of the Yankies, when it is hoped that the Emanations of the Leaden

George will make as deep impressions in the Bodies of some of his red Coated & Torie Subjects...." More plainly, the lead would be made into musket balls for patriot troops to shoot at the enemy.

But the work of turning King George into deadly projectiles couldn't be conducted in New York City. Every day more vessels carrying British troops and Hessian mercenaries, ultimately thirty thousand in all, sailed into New York Harbor, increasing the risk that the Continental Army might lose control of Manhattan and everything in it. (The British would in fact overrun Manhattan a little more than two months later.) A safe site for the work had to be found.

Thirty-nine-year-old Oliver Wolcott of Connecticut knew just the place: his hometown of Litchfield, deep in northwestern Connecticut, safe from British assault. Wolcott, as one of Connecticut's delegates to the Continental Congress in Philadelphia, was a strong supporter of the colonies severing all connection with Great Britain. Although sickness forced him to return to Connecticut before the final debate and vote on July 2 to declare independence, and the one on July 4 to approve the Declaration of Independence, he did later put his name to the document, becoming one of the revered signers.

On July 9, Wolcott was in New York, in command of a Connecticut militia unit preparing to defend the city against the impending British invasion. He arranged for King George's leaden remains to be transported to Litchfield, more than eighty miles as the crow flies from Manhattan— and a much longer distance by the available transportation at the time. The scraps were transported up the East River and into Long Island Sound on a sailing vessel. They were loaded onto carts in Norwalk, then dragged by oxen to their final destination, an apple orchard near Oliver Wolcott's spacious mansion on South Street in Litchfield.

There the lead was reportedly stored in a shed where Wolcott's nine-year-old son Frederick hacked it into manageable chunks with an axe. The work of casting the musket balls fell mostly to the women of the town, possibly because many of the men were serving in the army or the militia. These included Oliver Wolcott's own two daughters, Laura, fifteen, and Mary Ann, eleven, a Mrs. Marvin, a Ruth Marvin, a Mrs. Beach, and "sundry persons." Frederick Wolcott also took part.

The musket balls were made a few, or possibly only one, at a time. The work required first melting a small amount of lead in a ladle over an open fire. One tradition holds that some of the work was done in the kitchen fireplace of the Wolcott House, technically possible since the temperature of a wooden hearth fire could exceed the melting point of lead at 622 degrees Fahrenheit.

The molten lead was then poured into holes in a hinged metal tool that, once the lead hardened, could be opened to release the round projectiles. Any extruding excess lead would be clipped off. The result was a ball more than half an inch in diameter and weighing about three-quarters of an ounce.

However, the ladies of Litchfield apparently didn't just mold musket balls. Oliver Wolcott's records called their final product "cartridges." A "cartridge" was a rolled and twisted paper that contained a musket ball and enough gunpowder to shoot it. Soldiers in battle would tear off the top of a paper cartridge with their teeth, pour the gunpowder down the muzzle of the musket, then shove the musket ball and paper cartridge down the barrel with a ram rod. Using cartridges, which had everything needed to load a musket in a single package, was faster and more efficient than the alternative of measuring out a specific quantity of gunpowder from a powder horn, then pouring that down the barrel, followed by the ramming down of a musket ball wrapped in a cloth or paper "patch."

How long it took the ladies of Litchfield to work their way through the ton of metal sent from New York is unknown. But the final tally of their efforts amounted to 42,088 cartridges. The largest number produced by an individual was 11,592 cartridges made by Ruth Marvin. Mary Ann Wolcott turned out 10,790 cartridges, her younger sister Laura made 8,378, and Frederick produced 936.

Exactly when and to whom the musket balls were distributed isn't known for certain. Wolcott's accounting indicates that about three-quarters were "sent to court house." What building that refers to is unknown, but it apparently served as a site for stockpiling military materiel. Six hundred cartridges were given to the Litchfield militia, and 3,600 to the regiment of Colonel Edward Wigglesworth, who commanded troops at both the Battle of Saratoga, New York, and the Battle of Monmouth, New Jersey. Some of the cartridges may have been taken by Wolcott to the Battle of Saratoga, where he commanded troops.

However, it became evident that there was a discrepancy between the weight of the original statue and the amount of lead that reached Litchfield. The statue reportedly weighed about two tons, but the musket balls molded in Litchfield amounted to, approximately, only one ton of lead. Where was the rest of King George?

The royal head, at least, never left New York. Weighing fifty pounds, it was cut off, mutilated, and sent to a tavern near the patriot fortification of Fort Washington, farther north up Manhattan, with plans to fix it on a spike. However, a British soldier infiltrated the Continental Army lines and stole the head, which he buried to hide it. When the British took control of the area later that year, they exhumed the head and shipped it to England, where it arrived in late 1777.

At least ten more fragments, weighing together more than four hundred pounds, disappeared before the carts reached Litchfield. Some were likely pilfered during the carts' overnight stop at a tavern in what is today the town of Wilton, Connecticut, presumably by local residents who, remaining loyal to King George, wanted to keep as much of the lead as possible out of the hands of rebels who would make it into musket balls.

Some of these pieces were apparently buried or submerged in a local swamp for safekeeping. After half a century, some began to turn up on property that had originally been home to Loyalists. King George's arm surfaced in Wilton in 1991. It sold at auction in 2019 for more than $200,000.

Were the "melted majesty" musket balls fashioned in Litchfield ever fired in the war for American independence? That question was answered in part in 2015, when nine musket balls unearthed at the site of the 1778 Battle of Monmouth, New Jersey, in which New England troops commanded by Colonel Edmund Wigglesworth were among those who fought, were scientifically analyzed. The metallic composition of the balls closely matched that of surviving fragments of the statue of King George. The patriotic ladies of Litchfield had not labored in vain.

1780

The Dark Day

The darkness appeared in the western sky around daybreak and then approached steadily and ominously. By midday it blotted out the sun, making it impossible to work outdoors or read a newspaper inside. Chickens, fooled into thinking night had fallen, returned to their roosts, while nocturnal whippoorwills started to sing.

This may sound like a scene from an alien invasion horror movie—think *Independence Day*—but it actually happened in Connecticut. On a spring morning in 1780, the heavens turned mysteriously—and alarmingly—dark across much of the state.

Friday, May 19, dawned partly cloudy, with scattered light showers.

In Norwich the darkness first appeared around 8:00 a.m. By 11:00 a.m., a person "standing in the middle of a room furnished with 3 windows . . . could not read one word in a common newspaper," wrote attorney Benjamin Huntington.

In Thompson, about forty miles northeast of Norwich as the crow flew—or would have flown if the false nightfall hadn't sent him back to his nest—Joseph Joslin first noticed the darkness around 10:00 a.m., while he was building a stone wall. By noon, the gloom was so dense that Joslin couldn't see far enough to continue working.

He went inside, where candles had to be lit in order to see to prepare the midday meal. At that very hour similar conditions were recorded in New Haven, seventy miles southwest of Thompson, by Yale divinity professor Dr. Napthali Daggett.

In Hartford the Connecticut General Assembly was in session when the darkness began to manifest itself. Jedediah Strong of Litchfield, clerk of the House of Representatives, reached deep into his Yale graduate vocabulary for words impressive enough—although likely incomprehensible to the average man on the street—to describe the weird transformation. As Strong wrote in the Journal of the House, "A rolling, lowering sky, the vapours forming as it were an extensive concave integument in our hemisphere," created "a solemn gloom of unusual darkness" by 10:00 a.m. Conditions lightened briefly, "so that the sun became barely apparent through the heterogeneous penumbra."

Soon an even darker cloud arrived, so completely blocking the sun's rays that people couldn't read or write or even recognize each other at short distances. The House adjourned at 11:00 a.m.

But more was happening than just the mother of all clouds blotting out the sun in the sky. The phenomenon permeated the atmosphere at ground level, creating a creepy, unnatural effect.

In New Haven "unusual yellowness in the atmosphere made clean silver nearly resemble the color of brass," Dr. Daggett observed. "Every thing appeared to be Yellow" in Norwich, according to Benjamin Huntington. In Thompson "the air or clouds looked like brass," noted Joseph Joslin.

Legislators leaving the House chamber in Hartford encountered what Clerk Strong—in prose nearly as difficult to penetrate as the surrounding air—described as "circum-ambient exhalations of heterogeneous vapours in unequal columns of variegated smoke and fog, &c., waving in every direction, tinging one another and every visible object and dazzling the eye with glimmering coruscations of changeable green and yellow somewhat like the vibrating scaly shades of the aurora borealis."

Understandably, people were "anxiously enquiring for the cause and conjecturing the consequences of the rare and surprizing phoenomenon," according to House Clerk Strong. In rigorously religious Connecticut, founded by Puritans who believed everything happened according to the Lord's will, many people concluded that the darkness constituted at the very least a warning from an unquestionably unhappy God.

Some feared the darkness was a much more momentous sign, that in fact it heralded the coming of Judgment Day. That possibility was raised in Hartford in the Governor's Council, the forerunner of the modern State Senate. With the House of Representatives having already shut down, it was proposed that the Governor's Council do the same. But a cooler head prevailed in the General Assembly's upper chamber.

That head belonged to sixty-five-year-old Abraham Davenport of Stamford. Davenport spoke against adjourning, observing with classic Yankee common sense, "The day of judgment is either approaching, or it is not. If it is not, there is no cause for an adjournment; if it is, I choose to be found doing my duty." He suggested that candles be lit, and the Council carried on with its business.

Davenport's display of calm wisdom in the midst of people beset by end-of-the-world jitters was written into New England lore by the popular poet John Greenleaf Whittier. In the poem "Abraham Davenport," published eighty-six years after the darkness, Whittier memorialized him as "A witness to the ages as they pass / That simple duty hath no place for fear."

In most locations the darkness lasted around an hour. By early afternoon the skies were clearing. The House of Representatives reconvened at 2:00 p.m.

Relief swept the state when the apocalypse did not follow the darkness. Many people nonetheless considered it a message from the Almighty, despite assurances like that of Dr. Naphtali Daggett that "there is no reason to consider it as supernatural or ominous" nor to "be in the least terrified by it."

Others sought a scientific explanation. "The particular cause of this phaenomenon, we must leave to astronomers to determine," observed the *New London Gazette*. Seeking hard evidence to use in determining the true nature of the darkness, the *Connecticut Courant* on May 23 asked "our ingenious and philosophical customers . . . to send an account of the particular phoenomena attending it, in their respective places—particularly an exact description of the time of its beginning, continuance and end—the appearance and tincture of the clouds, and other visible objects."

Reports from observers outside Connecticut were used to try to determine the cause of what became known as the Dark Day, which affected some part of every New England state and neighboring New York, as well as New Jersey. There were accounts of the darkness being accompanied by rain that had the smell, taste, and color of burned leaves, and by black ash which coated the surface of standing water.

These clues and others, including the opaqueness of the air and the strange hues observed in Connecticut, resulted in the theory that the Dark Day was the result of smoke from forest fires in wilderness areas of New York, New Hampshire, New Jersey, Canada—or all four.

It's a plausible explanation, but the cause of the Dark Day has yet to be definitely determined.

1781

Massacre at Fort Griswold

When a messenger spreading the call to arms arrived before dawn on September 6, 1781, Elnathan Perkins, sixty-three, set out from his home in Groton, Connecticut, for Fort Griswold on the eastern bank of the Thames River. Joining him there in response to the alarm were his four sons: Obadiah, forty-one; Elisha, thirty-five; Asa, thirty-three; and Luke, twenty-nine.

They soon learned what was behind the urgent summons: Two dozen British ships had appeared in Long Island Sound and were preparing to land troops for an assault on Fort Griswold and on New London across the river.

Elnathan, Elisha, Asa, and Luke Perkins would not live to see the sun set that day. They were among the more than eighty patriot defenders killed in the military engagement that has gone down in Connecticut history as the Battle of Groton Heights or, more graphically, the Massacre at Fort Griswold.

The Connecticut coast had suffered several British raids since the outbreak of the Revolution, including ones at Norwalk, Fairfield, and New Haven. These had resulted in widespread destruction of property from fire and looting, but relatively few deaths. This time the outcome would be much more devastating.

New London was headquarters to Connecticut's small naval force, and its harbor was home to many privateers—private ships that in time of war were granted government permission to seize enemy vessels and bring them into port. This "legalized piracy" inflicted more damage on the British fleet than did the patriots' tiny navy, for privateer crews were motivated by the fact that they received a portion of the value of any ship and cargo they brought into port.

As a result, New London and Groton had always been prime candidates for a British raid. On September 6, 1781, they were particularly ripe for the picking. Four heavily armed privateers were in port, and several recently captured British ships, including the most valuable one ever seized by a Connecticut privateer, were anchored in the Thames. Large quantities of supplies, many taken from captured enemy vessels, were stored in New London warehouses.

One other factor contributed to the British decision to launch an assault on Groton and New London and also made the confrontation extremely personal. Benedict Arnold, the native of nearby Norwich who a year earlier had turned traitor and deserted from the Continental Army to sign on with the British, had lobbied hard for such an invasion. He was in command of the more than 1,700 troops that landed that day.

The enemy came ashore at mid-morning and split into two forces, each containing about eight hundred soldiers. The one under Arnold began marching up the west bank of the harbor toward New London; the other advanced up the opposite side toward Fort Griswold, a patriot garrison.

The enemy progressed swiftly up the western bank of the Thames. Upon reaching New London, Arnold ordered that warehouses containing supplies be set ablaze. Before long, private homes and buildings were also being torched. Soon nearly the entire town, along with a number of vessels anchored in the river, was engulfed in flames. When the ashes had cooled, it was calculated that 143 structures had been destroyed.

On the Groton side of the Thames, the scenario played out differently. British troops came within sight of Fort Griswold but then stopped.

Fort Griswold, commanded by Colonel William Ledyard, had stone walls ten to twelve feet tall, from the top of which protruded tree trunks with branches that had been sharpened so as to impale or at least impede anyone who tried to scale them. A wide defensive ditch also surrounded the outside of the fort. By noontime the soldiers on active duty were joined by enough volunteers to bring their total strength to 158, including Elnathan Perkins and his four sons.

The British dispatched men under a flag of truce to meet with representatives of the patriot garrison. The British called for the fort to surrender immediately. That demand was carried to Fort Griswold, and soon word came back that the fortification would not be given up to the British.

The redcoats now had another message for the defenders of Fort Griswold: If the British had to fight a battle to capture the fort, there would be "no quarter"—no mercy—for the defenders. Anybody who survived the assault would be killed. Colonel Ledyard replied, "We will not give up the fort, let the consequences be what they may."

The British launched their attack on Fort Griswold. The American defenders fought with courage and deadly effect. But Fort Griswold had not been kept in good condition, and the patriots, few of whom had combat experience, were outnumbered five to one by professional, trained, battle-tested British soldiers. It was only a matter of time before enemy troops began to force their way into the fort.

Colonel Ledyard, realizing that further resistance was futile, ordered his men to cease fighting, but many couldn't hear him over the noise of battle. "According to the best intelligence I have been able to collect," Connecticut Governor Jonathan Trumbull wrote to George Washington just nine days after the battle, Colonel Ledyard "thought proper to surrender himself with the garrison prisoners, and accordingly presented his sword to a British officer on the parade, who received the same and immediately thrust it through that brave but unfortunate commander."

Within seconds, Fort Griswold was transformed from a battlefield to a slaughterhouse. British victors, seized by a gory frenzy, either shot or bayoneted more than 120 patriot defenders. It was not simply a case of fulfilling the threat of "no quarter." The wounded and men already dead were stabbed and slashed again and again. Corpses were mutilated so badly that loved ones later could barely recognize them.

The story of Colonel Ledyard being skewered with his own sword that had been communicated to Governor

Trumbull became the stuff of legend—even though Trumbull cautioned in his letter to Washington that "many material circumstances relative to the tragical scene are not yet obtainable with such a degree of precision and certainty as might be wished"—that is, not all the facts of the battle were in or verified. However, examination of surviving physical evidence—the linen vest Ledyard was wearing when he was killed—suggests the fatal wound was more likely the result of a bayonet thrust into Ledyard's side, calling into question the accuracy of the report sent to Trumbull.

Why had British soldiers degenerated so suddenly into savages? One explanation was that they were infuriated at the unexpectedly stubborn fight put up by the fort's garrison. Another possibility put forth was that the British had seen the fort's flag come down and assumed it was a sign of surrender. In fact, a bullet had cut through the rope holding the flag aloft, causing it to fall. It was quickly put back up, but some redcoats were convinced that it had been a ruse to deceive them.

By the time the British bloodlust had been slaked, eighty-five patriots were dead, and another thirty-five had been wounded, some fatally. When they sailed away the next morning, the British carried off some of the survivors as prisoners of war; the most seriously wounded were left behind.

Precisely how Elnathan, Asa, Elisha, and Luke Perkins died was not recorded. They were buried near one another in Starr Cemetery. The eldest Perkins son, Obadiah, suffered wounds from three bayonet thrusts but survived the day.

The grieving families of the Perkinses and other fallen defenders erected tombstones in graveyards in Groton and the northern half of the present-day town of Ledyard. They were determined that the despicable manner in which the men had died should never be forgotten. Perhaps the epitaph for nineteen-year-old Benadam Allyn best sums up this urge to have their sacrifice remembered.

> To future ages this shall Tell
> This brave youth in fort griswould fell

Similar references were chiseled into more than three dozen gravestones. Particularly explicit and graphic was the epitaph that reads:

> Killed in fort Griswould after he Surrendered sept 6th 1781
> My blood was spilt upon ye Earth By Relentless Inhuman foes
> Will not a day of reckoning come
> does not my blood for vengeance cry
> how will those wretches bear their doom

Elnathan Perkins's stone recounted the enormous tragedy that had befallen his family, lamenting that,

> Ye British Power that boast aloud
> of your Great Lenity [clemency],
> behold my fate when at your feet
> I and three Sons must Die.

Elisha Perkins's gravestone inscription reports that he "fell a Sacrifice for his Countrys Cause in that horrible massacre at fort Griswould sept 6th 1781." Luke Perkins's stone proclaims

> Ye sons of Liberty be not Dismayd
> That I have fell a Sacrifice to Death.
> But oh to think how will this debt be paid
> Who murthered me when they are called from earth.

Asa Perkins's epitaph spoke of "British tyrants" and "butchers wet with Humane Gore." Other vividly descriptive phrases in epitaphs included "Inhumanly Massacred by British troops," "british Inhumanity," "sacrifice to british Barbarity," "the Victim of ungenerous Rage and Cruelty," "horrible Massacre," and "victim to British cruelty."

Although Benedict Arnold had been nowhere near Fort Griswold, many blamed the despised turncoat for the carnage. Epitaphs referred to the "Bloody Massacre at Fort Griswould committed by Benedict Arnolds troops" and, in several cases, to "Traitor Arnold's murdering corps."

In 1830 the State of Connecticut erected near the site of Fort Griswold a 127-foot-tall monument, topped by a soaring granite obelisk, to commemorate the defenders. Its height was later increased by seven feet. Today the site of the massacre is Fort Griswold Battlefield State Park. It is listed on the National Register of Historic Places. Timeworn fortifications, including stone walls, ditches, and earthworks bear mute tribute to the many men and boys who died to defend them.

1789

George Washington's Inauguration Suit

Clothes can make much more than just a fashion statement. What a person wears can send all manner of messages, including political ones. That is what George Washington was deliberately doing when he donned a solid brown suit made from woolen cloth manufactured in Connecticut for one of the most important events not just of his life but of that of the new nation: his inauguration as the first president of the United States.

Washington had led the Continental Army to an almost miraculous victory in the American Revolution, securing independence from British governmental control. In the war's waning days, some people suggested Washington should become king of the United States—an idea Washington firmly rejected. He resigned as commander-in-chief and returned to private life at Mount Vernon in Virginia.

Washington only reluctantly agreed to accept the presidency when it became clear that the controversial new U.S. Constitution's best chance of success was for Washington, the man trusted by more Americans than any other, to head the new government. On February 4, 1789, the members of the Electoral College cast their ballots unanimously for Washington as president—the only man ever so honored. That vote was little more than a formality, given that everyone—including Washington—knew that his election was a foregone conclusion. The inauguration was set for April 30, 1789, in New York City, then the temporary capital of the United States.

Washington understood the power of clothing to communicate. When he represented Virginia in the Second Continental Congress, which convened shortly after the American Revolution had erupted at Lexington and Concord in April 1775, he had attended every session in the smart, colorful uniform he had worn as a colonel in the Virginia militia. It was a silent but unmistakable announcement of his willingness to serve in a military capacity—a tacit offer Congress took up when it appointed him commander of the Continental Army that June.

For his momentous swearing-in as president fourteen years later, Washington chose to wear neither a martial uniform nor the robes of nobility. When he stepped out onto the balcony of Federal Hall to take the oath of office, he was dressed as an ordinary civilian, appropriate for a leader who had been elevated to his office by the vote of the people.

Washington had hoped that his inauguration-day outfit would send a second message: that political independence from Great Britain would mean little to Americans if they continued to rely on foreign countries for so many of the goods they used, including cloth.

As a colonial Virginia planter, Washington had learned firsthand the dangers of being dependent on imports. Great Britain had deliberately suppressed manufacturing in its colonies to keep them from competing with British firms. As a result, colonists could obtain a vast array of products—from first-rate clothing to farm implements to glass—only from foreign sources, most often British.

Goods arriving from abroad often were of inferior quality and overpriced, but Washington had no choice but to accept them. He and many other southern planters found themselves chronically in debt to foreign suppliers.

With the outbreak of the Revolution, the powerful British navy shut down most American trade with Europe. The rebellious colonists were thrown upon their own resources to clothe themselves and the men fighting for American independence. There were, of course, no factories, so the task of filling the garment gap fell to the ordinary men and women who had all along been making the homespun clothes Americans wore for work and everyday activities. They proved up to the challenge, doing the tedious, time-consuming work of producing fabric and fashioning it into shirts, coats, pants, and blankets by the tens of thousands in Connecticut alone.

Homespun goods did the job of covering the human body, but typically they were rough in quality, especially when compared with the first-rate European manufactured goods that had been available before the war. With the conflict's end in 1783, trade with Europe resumed, and Americans eagerly returned to buying imported cloth.

Even then, Washington worried that dependence on foreign suppliers would leave the new nation vulnerable to any enemy that could disrupt trade, and he foresaw the need for Americans to become self-sufficient. At his inauguration six years later, he was able to make that point thanks to a visionary enterprise that had started up just a year earlier in Connecticut.

Perhaps with his upcoming swearing-in already in mind, Washington was excited to read an ad headlined "American Woolens" in the January 29, 1789, issue of the *New York Daily Advertiser* newspaper. It announced that Gilbert Everingham in New York City had "Just received from the flourishing Manufactory at Hartford, a few Pieces of superfine BROADCLOTHS, of an excellent quality."

That "flourishing Manufactory," as Washington would soon learn, was actually a speculative venture of an old army acquaintance, Jeremiah Wadsworth of Hartford. A wealthy merchant in civilian life, Wadsworth for much of the Revolution had successfully handled the difficult job of keeping supplies flowing to the Continental Army and its allies. Wadsworth, too, appreciated the need for Americans to become self-sufficient, and he also was exploring innovative investments. In 1788 he and a group of investors had established the Hartford Woolen Manufactory, the first wool factory in the United States. The cloth offered for sale in the New York newspaper was among its initial output.

Washington, still in Virginia, wrote to another fellow veteran, Henry Knox, in New York, asking him to buy enough of the Hartford-made cloth to make a suit. Washington left the choice of color—either "London Smoke" or "Hartford Grey"—to Knox. He suggested, however, that if the cloth hadn't been expertly dyed or if the fabric should not be as good as he hoped, then Knox should opt for whichever less readily showed the imperfections. Washington stated his belief that America was overdue in throwing off British influences as well as his hope that it would soon be considered a fashion faux pas for a man to wear clothing not made in the United States.

When Wadsworth and his fellow investors got wind of the future president's interest in their product, they smelled a unique promotional opportunity for their fledgling factory that had to be seized quickly. They offered to provide Washington with the material for his inaugural suit, hinting that if he wore the suit, it would do wonders for advancing the cause of American manufacturing.

They even sent him fabric swatches to select from. Washington chose brown.

When the cloth arrived from Hartford, Washington was pleasantly surprised to find that the quality of the fabric was even better than he had dared hope. He considered the success of the Hartford Woolen Manufactory an encouraging sign that the country would be able to supply itself with quality cloth that would be competitively priced with imports. The fabric was quickly made up into a suit, with gilt buttons stamped with eagles.

Thanks to the Hartford Woolen Manufactory, when George Washington took his oath of office as president, he wore a suit that not only declared the supremacy of the civilian authority in a democracy but also was an endorsement of American-made products. The latter message got through loud and clear. The president's sartorial selection was noted in many newspapers. On May 5, 1789, the *New York Packet*'s coverage of the inauguration reported, "We feel a satisfaction ... that his Excellency [as the president was then styled] on that great day, was dressed in a complete suit of elegant broadcloth of the manufacture of his country."

It wasn't enough that Wadsworth and his fellow investors had put Hartford Woolen Manufactory cloth on the president's back. The *Salem Mercury* newspaper of March 31, 1789, reported that John Adams "has lately received an elegant suit of AMERICAN BROADCLOTH manufactured at Hartford, in which he will make his appearance as vice-president of the United States." Jeremiah Wadsworth himself, who had been elected to represent Connecticut in the U.S. House of Representatives, and Oliver Ellsworth, one of the state's first U.S. senators, also sported suits of Hartford cloth.

Washington gave another boost to the Hartford Woolen Manufactory by visiting it when he was in Connecticut that autumn as part of a presidential tour of New England. The State of Connecticut provided tangible support in the form of economic incentives, such as bounties on yarn spun and made into cloth, multiyear tax breaks for both the factory and its employees, and even permission to hold a lottery to raise funding.

Ultimately, all the patriotic enthusiasm and government subsidies in the world couldn't make up for the myriad disadvantages under which the Hartford Woolen Manufactory was forced to operate, including the lack of modern equipment (the British refused to allow their textile machinery to be exported), trained and experienced craftsmen, and quality raw material. The company was unable to produce cloth of comparable quality to that available from Europe and couldn't compete on price. In 1795 the Hartford Woolen Manufactory went out of business.

What happened to that suit made with such high hopes for George Washington to wear at his inauguration? That's a mystery. Washington's Mount Vernon home has a coat of woolen broadcloth that belonged to the first President. However, since research has been unable to prove conclusively that this was the Hartford-produced garment Washington had on when he was sworn in, Mount Vernon says only that it was "possibly" worn at the inauguration.

Despite the failure of the Hartford Woolen Manufactory, the core principle of made-in-America remained very much alive. Within a few decades Connecticut would become one of the most important manufacturing centers for many of the items that America needed, from clocks to guns to swords— and cloth, fulfilling the vision that had prompted George Washington to wear that suit of Hartford wool.

1796

The First American Cookbook

The first generation of American women to come of age following the Revolution had their own version of Betty Crocker in Amelia Simmons. Simmons's *American Cookery*, published in Hartford in 1796, was the first compilation of recipes and culinary advice written by an American to meet the unique needs of the new nation's kitchens.

Cookbooks then available had been penned mostly by Englishwomen. For her work Simmons "borrowed" many of the traditional recipes included in these books. She "adapted to this country" some of these recipes by substituting for key ingredients foods unknown before the discovery of North America, including turkey, pumpkin, and corn. These had been afforded little attention in previously available English cookbooks.

Corn, to which the first European settlers had been introduced by Native Americans, was a staple of the ordinary person's daily diet in the 1700s in British North America. It was called "Indian corn," because at that time the word "corn" alone referred to any grain.

Indian corn was not the familiar sweet corn eaten fresh on the cob (a variety that didn't become common on American dinner tables until the 1840s), but more like what today is called "field corn." Simmons's recipes for a "Nice Indian Pudding," "Johny Cake," and "Indian Slapjack" all used Indian corn ground into meal.

Simmons's recipe for that historic American holiday classic, pumpkin pie, called for combining a quart of milk, a pint of "pompkin" (standardization of spelling was still some years in the future), four eggs, and unspecified amounts of molasses, allspice, and ginger. The mixture was put into a crust and baked for an hour.

Simmons offered two recipes for stuffing for a roast turkey. To a pound of soft wheat bread, three ounces of beef suet, three eggs, thyme, marjoram, pepper, and salt, "some add a gill [about five ounces] of wine," she advised. As a side dish to the turkey, she suggested "cramberry" sauce.

Simmons also pioneered the inclusion in printed recipes of an American forerunner of baking powder called "pearl ash." "Pearl ash" is concentrated, purified potash, a substance derived from hardwood ash soaked in water. As unappetizing as its origin might sound, pearl ash revolutionized baking. It made cakes and breads rise. Previously leavening was achieved only by using much slower acting yeast or whipped egg whites, or by prolonged kneading of dough.

Beyond being a pioneering work of American cuisine, *American Cookery* documents the cooking practices and available foods of Americans more than two centuries ago—and in some cases illustrates how drastically they have changed. To whip up the popular drink called syllabub, Simmons directed the cook to sweeten a quart of cider with sugar, spice it with grated nutmeg, and "then milk your cow" into it.

A modern mainstream cookbook is unlikely to include anything resembling Simmons's recipe for how to "dress a calve's head." After scalding the head, it was split open, and the brains were removed. The brains were washed, seasoned, and diced, and then stirred into what Simmons called "the whole mess in the pot," which was a stewlike concoction made of meat from the boiled calf's head and feet, to which fried meatballs made of veal and pork had been added.

The origin of the name for pound cake becomes clear from one of Simmons's recipes, which called for "one pound sugar, one pound butter, one pound flour, one pound or ten eggs." The cake was flavored, not with vanilla, which was just being introduced into the United States, but with rose water. Easily prepared at home by steeping fresh rose petals in water, rose water was included among the ingredients in several of Simmons's recipes for cakes, puddings, custard, and even an apple pie.

Simmons wrote her book for a specific audience: "those females in this country, who by the loss of their parents, or other unfortunate circumstances, are reduced to the necessity of going into families in the line of domestics, or taking refuge with their friends or relations, and doing those things which are really essential to the perfecting them as good wives, and useful members to society." She knew that audience intimately, for as the cover of *American Cookery* proclaimed she herself was "an American orphan," someone who had not learned the basics of cooking in the traditional way, working alongside her mother or another female relative.

The target audience determined *American Cookery*'s format: simple, utilitarian, affordable. Forty-seven pages long (compared to English cookbooks that ran to more than three hundred pages), seven inches high, printed on untrimmed paper bound by string, it would be considered a pamphlet by today's standards. It featured no illustrations to make the reader's mouth water or to inspire the ambitious cook and no detailed "how-to" diagrams. It sold for the equivalent of a couple of dollars.

Even with Simmons's pioneering book to guide her, a woman who lacked the benefit of an experienced adviser would have to endure a considerable amount of trial and error before becoming a skilled cook. Some of Simmons's recipes were vague about the amounts of each ingredient to include. Her potato cake recipe called for potatoes, egg yolks, wine, melted butter, and flour, with no hint as to how much of each to use or how the quantities of the ingredients related to one another. If she used five pounds of potatoes, for example, how many egg yolks or how much wine would she need to add? Only repeated experimentation could answer those critical questions.

Even when some specifics were offered, they were of limited help in an era before the easy availability of standardized measuring spoons or cups. Calling for "a coffee cup full of boiled and strained carrots," as Simmons did in one recipe, or "two spoons of flour," as she did in another, was imprecise at best, since, for example, one cook's spoon might be the size of a modern teaspoon, another's the size of a modern tablespoon.

Its occasional vagueness notwithstanding, *American Cookery* was so wildly popular that before the year was out Simmons had to publish a second edition to meet the demand. This one, however, was printed in Albany, New York, because, Simmons claimed, the Hartford publisher had botched the original printing, allowing errors to creep into her text and adding an entire section that she had not written.

American Cookery was reprinted in Hartford in 1798, but by a Northampton, Massachusetts, publisher. It remained in print for more than three decades.

It was issued in a number of editions in Vermont and New Hampshire as well as in Connecticut, New York, New Jersey, and Massachusetts. Some of those reprints omitted Simmons's name from the book.

Betty Crocker and Amelia Simmons are alike in the perennial popularity of the publications bearing their names. (The Betty Crocker cookbook has sold more than seventy-five million copies since its first publication in 1950.) And they are also similar in another way: Betty Crocker is not a real person, and no one knows who Amelia Simmons truly was—or if there even was an Amelia Simmons.

Betty Crocker is a persona invented in 1921 to serve as the public, human face of one of the six Minnesota flour companies that would soon merge to form General Mills, which made Betty their icon. As for Amelia Simmons, apart from the authorship appearing on *American Cookery*'s cover and the statement of the book's copyright, historians have been unable to locate any documented evidence of her. The name may have been a pseudonym adopted for some unknown reason by the author or authors of the book. To this day, the true identity of the author of *American Cookery* remains an American mystery.

But the significance of the crude pamphlet published by a still-unidentified author is undeniable. The Library of Congress included *American Cookery* on its list of eighty-eight "Books that Shaped America." A writer for Feeding America: Historic American Cookbook Project, summed up its significance with the statement that, "The importance of this work cannot be overestimated. Its initial publication (Hartford, 1796) was, in its own way, a second Declaration of American Independence."

1796–1810

Perkins's Tractors

Was Dr. Elisha Perkins a clever quack who suckered tens of thousands of dupes, or a sincere, if quixotic, would-be healer? That question still lingers more than two centuries after the Connecticut physician invented a device that reportedly relieved severe pain and cured ailments ranging from gout to epileptic seizures. Perkins's tractors were in hot demand on both sides of the Atlantic for nearly a decade—until skeptics succeeded in debunking them.

Elisha Perkins was no traveling snake-oil salesman. Born in 1741 in Lisbon in eastern Connecticut, he was the son of a doctor, from whom Elisha probably received his medical training.

Dr. Perkins settled in nearby Plainfield and proceeded to practice medicine for more than thirty years, earning the respect and trust of his patients and colleagues. He was one of the incorporators of the Connecticut Medical Society in 1792. Along the way he married and fathered five sons and five daughters.

During his career as a country physician, Dr. Perkins made several curious observations. During a surgical procedure he noticed that the touch of a metal instrument caused a muscle to contract, whereas instruments made of other materials had no effect. He also observed, according to his son Benjamin, that "a cessation of pain had ensued when a knife or lancet was applied to separate the gum from a tooth, preparatory to extracting it," and that "momentary ease was given in a few instances, by the accidental application of a metallic instrument to inflamed and painful tumours, previous to any incision."

Dr. Perkins concluded that metal had a unique effect on tissue. By 1795, after several years of experimentation, he developed a medical device designed specifically to apply the healing and pain-relieving power of metal. Called "Perkins's tractors," it actually comprised two parts—a pair of plain metal rods, about three inches long, each made from a different secret combination of metals. The tractors were flat on one side, concave on the other, tapering from a rounded head to a sharp point. When they were drawn or "traced"— hence the name "tractors"—across the ailing part of a body, pain and the debilitating symptoms of diseases such as rheumatism often vanished.

On February 19, 1796, Dr. Perkins obtained a federal patent for "removing pains and inflammations from the human body, by the application of metallic substances." Not surprisingly, many greeted his new device with skepticism. In May 1796 the Connecticut Medical Society denounced Perkins's tractors as "delusive quackery" that had been "gleaned up from the miserable remains of animal magnetism."

The reference was to the Austrian physician Friedrich Mesmer, who had experimented with magnets to treat illness before deciding that the power he called "animal magnetism" existed within his own body. For several years in Paris, Mesmer enjoyed a high-profile and highly profitable career of "healing" with animal magnetism by simply passing his hands above a patient. After a royal committee of scientists declared Mesmer a fraud, he fell into disgrace.

Dr. Perkins wasn't deterred by his colleagues' barbed criticism. He traveled to Philadelphia, then the capital of the United States, to demonstrate his tractors in hospitals and before members of Congress. President George Washington himself reportedly purchased a set. Dr. Perkins published testimonials to the tractors' effectiveness supplied by physicians, ministers, and laymen. The Reverend Micaiah Porter of Voluntown, Connecticut, wrote that by using Perkins's tractors "I have almost invariably succeeded to my own astonishment, in curing head-achs, teeth-achs, rheumatisms and burns." Dr. Samuel Willard of Stafford, Connecticut, reported "very happy success" in treating a case of acute rheumatism that he and several other physicians had been unable to relieve by any other means.

Like any clever Yankee, Dr. Perkins sought to turn a much-needed dollar from his invention. Physicians in that era earned about the same as blacksmiths or tavern keepers, and Dr. Perkins, whose wife had recently died leaving him with three children still under sixteen, had chronic money problems. Thus the doctor became an enterprising salesman and promoter. He traveled throughout New England and the middle Atlantic states, selling tractors himself, selling them in bulk to others for resale, and licensing individuals to use them. He warned potential customers to accept no substitute for the "original and genuine" Perkins's tractors, implying that their power came from their unique design and secret metallic makeup.

Within a year of securing his patent, Dr. Perkins's tractors were being marketed from Maine to Delaware. An idea of their popularity can be gleaned from the fact that during the last six months of 1796 alone, a local clock maker fashioned more than four thousand pairs of tractors for Dr. Perkins.

Testimonials and enthusiastic customers didn't impress the members in attendance at the Connecticut Medical Society's meeting in May 1797. Dr. Perkins was voted out of the organization, a rejection that pained him little if at all. He continued to energetically market his tractors, making trips into the southern states. By 1798 he had met with so much success that he was contemplating moving from small, rural Plainfield to a major city from which he could manage his medical supply venture more profitably.

Late in 1797 Dr. Perkins's son Benjamin, fresh out of Yale, arrived in England, where he patented and promoted the tractors. Around the same time the wife of a Danish official in the United States took a pair of tractors back to her home country. Experiments conducted by physicians at the royal hospital in Copenhagen supported the effectiveness of the tractors.

These findings about the medical treatment that in Europe came to be called "Perkinism" were published in a book that was later translated into German and English. The tractors quickly became even more popular in Europe than they had been in North America—and equally as controversial.

During 1798 Dr. Perkins used his tractors along with special dietary restrictions and requirements, including an elixir made of sea salt and vinegar, to treat yellow fever patients in several cities. The results left him confident that the combination constituted a quick and easy cure for the deadly disease.

That possibility must have been personally gratifying to Dr. Perkins, who had lost a daughter, a son-in-law, and two grandchildren in the horrific 1793 yellow fever epidemic that killed five thousand people in Philadelphia—about one-tenth of the city's population. No one then knew how the disease was transmitted (through the bite of a mosquito) or how to prevent or cure it—which was the case for almost all illnesses at that time, when medicine was in its infancy as a science. Dr. Benjamin Rush, one of the nation's most eminent physicians, had tried in vain to treat victims of the 1793 Philadelphia epidemic with bleeding, laxatives, and induced vomiting—a regimen Dr. Perkins considered ridiculous.

Dr. Perkins vowed that if yellow fever broke out in a major city, he would risk his life to help its victims. He got his chance to do just that in the summer of 1799, when a significant number of yellow fever cases began to be reported in New York City.

By July 31, 1799, Dr. Elisha Perkins was in the city, advertising his services to cure yellow fever. On Friday, August 30, he himself came down with symptoms of the disease. Dr. Perkins at first treated himself; whether he used his tractors is unknown, although he did have a number of sets with him.

When the illness didn't respond to his own treatment, Dr. Perkins agreed to have another physician called in. At first the consulting doctor's treatment resulted in no improvement, but on Monday Dr. Perkins began to feel better—only to have a drastic relapse on Wednesday night. Such a temporary improvement was a common characteristic of yellow fever.

The outside physician was again summoned, but nothing he tried helped the obviously terminal patient. Dr. Elisha Perkins, fifty-eight, died on September 6, 1799, of the very disease he had hoped to defeat.

Given that yellow fever had claimed so many victims and that the nature of its transmission was unknown, the corpses of those who succumbed to it were interred as quickly as possible. Dr. Perkins was buried in a newly opened potter's field where today stands Washington Square Park—a site then on the fringe of the city. He probably lies there still, for when the city converted the site into a park in 1825, it simply brought in fill to cover the estimated twenty thousand bodies the graveyard by then contained.

Dr. Elisha Perkins might be dead, but Perkinism thrived in Europe for a few years longer. The debunking of Perkins's tractors began in 1800, when English physicians published a report claiming they had achieved the same results using tractors made of wood painted to look like metal. Other doubters performed experiments demonstrating that sham tractors made of wax or bone also proved as effective as metal ones. Before the decade was over, Perkins's tractors had passed from medical miracle to quaint curiosity.

Benjamin Perkins returned to the United States in 1803, not to his native Connecticut, but to the city where his father had died. He had amassed a considerable amount of money during his five years marketing tractors in Europe. He became a prominent New Yorker, known for his philanthropy among other things, before his death in 1810 at just thirty-six years old.

And what about Dr. Elisha Perkins? Whether he believed that only his specially crafted tractors possessed the power to heal or whether he made that claim to maximize sales seems open to question. But that he honestly had faith in his invention is strongly supported by his willingness to gamble his own life by knowingly exposing himself to yellow fever in order to treat its victims with his tractors.

1796–1850

Good for Whatever Ails Ya

Two centuries ago "biliousness" was the vague catchall diagnosis for a broad spectrum of gastrointestinal symptoms, from constipation to appendicitis. For generations of Americans, the cure-all for this slightly silly-sounding condition, as well as an assortment of other ailments, was the first medicine ever patented in the United States: pills formulated by Dr. Samuel Lee, Jr., of Windham, Connecticut.

When Dr. Lee, just twenty-three, took out a patent on his new drug in 1796, there were no pharmaceutical companies or research institutions employing teams of scientists to spend years developing new medications. There were just individual physicians like Dr. Lee, who drew on the combination of centuries-old superstition and speculation that constituted most of that era's "medical" knowledge, their imagination, and their experience treating patients to develop their own remedies.

In addition to biliousness, Dr. Lee claimed that his pills effectively treated the "gravel" (kidney stones), "dropsy" (excessive fluid retention), and what were modestly referred to as "female complaints." Supposedly they were also "very efficacious in preventing the yellow fever."

Although Dr. Lee must have believed that his pills were special enough to go to the trouble of patenting them, he did not, unlike most inventors of a new medicine, keep the ingredients a secret. The pills were composed of gamboges (the juices of trees from Southeast Asia), aloes (the juices of aloe plants from the Caribbean), soap, and nitrate of potassa (also known as saltpeter—which is an ingredient in gunpowder).

A pill containing these four components would cause a patient to vomit, move his bowels, sweat excessively, and urinate frequently. Producing such forceful and unpleasant purging was in line with the prevailing medical "wisdom" that disease resulted from an imbalance of fluids in the body, including bile secreted by the liver—hence the term "bilious."

"Lee's Windham bilious pills," as they were marketed, might conceivably have been helpful to a small number of patients, such as a person suffering from constipation alone or a child who had ingested a poisonous substance. In most cases, however, they would have done nothing more than increase the sick person's physical discomfort.

Depending on the true nature of the patient's illness, the pills might have made things worse or even led to death. Nonetheless, Dr. Lee's pills were less likely to harm or kill a patient than many other concoctions on the market because, as their inventor emphasized, they did not contain mercury. That poisonous metal, which can lead to mental impairment, blindness, and even death, is a powerful laxative and also was a key ingredient in many medicines in the 1700s and 1800s.

Lee's Windham bilious pills quickly became popular, thanks in part to their inventor's energetic and innovative marketing and distribution strategy. Dr. Lee packaged his pills in distinctive wrappers, advertised them in newspapers, and supplied them to pharmacists, physicians, and other retailers for resale. He might be considered a forerunner of the modern pharmaceutical industry, which wouldn't truly emerge for another twenty-five years.

By the end of 1797, Lee's Windham bilious pills were being sold in stores from Vermont to South Carolina. Dr. Lee reported that one Boston store alone sold nearly ten thousand boxes in just two years.

Then, in the summer of 1798, things got complicated for Dr. Lee—very complicated. Advertisements began appearing in newspapers for Lee's bilious pills, but with a small yet crucial difference.

These ads were for New London, not Windham, bilious pills, and they were produced by Samuel H. P. Lee, a druggist in New London, just twenty miles south of Windham. Purportedly, the New London pills not only were good for all the illnesses treated by the Windham pills but also could cure worms, partial palsy, rheumatism, hysterical afflictions, and convulsions.

Dr. Lee of Windham saw this as an unprincipled attempt by the New London Lee to take unfair advantage of their nearly identical names to profit from the physician's successful patented medicine. He immediately took his case to the public via newspaper advertisements, claiming that Samuel H. P. Lee had been a retailer of the Windham pills for about a year but had quit after Dr. Lee refused to supply him with pills on the terms he wanted. The New London Lee then, according to Dr. Lee, "fabricated certain pills, resembling in appearance" the Windham bilious pills, "but of different ingredients."

He allegedly copied Dr. Lee's promotional copy and advertising program, warned people against buying Lee's Windham bilious pills, and published a fraudulent testimonial to his New London pills. Dr. Lee called Samuel H. P. Lee "capable of measures so wicked, to defraud an individual, and so mean to impose on the public."

Thus was touched off a war of words that would be played out in the newspapers. A week later Samuel H. P. Lee called Dr. Lee of Windham a teller of "dirty falsehoods," a man beset by "folly and ignorance." Dr. Lee of Windham resorted to emphasizing in his newspaper ads in giant type that his were the "True & Genuine Bilious Pills."

Samuel H. P. Lee contended that his pills were not identical in composition to those made in Windham, and that Dr. Lee's failure to take legal action for patent infringement was a tacit acknowledgment that he knew his case had no merit. The charges that flew back and forth accomplished little except perhaps, as one historian suggests, to raise the visibility of both types of Lee's bilious pills, to the profit of both men.

In 1799 Samuel H. P. Lee solved the patent question by taking out a patent of his own for bilious pills. In the spring of that year, he also became a doctor, adding further to the confusion for customers.

Both men tried to distinguish their product by distinctive packaging, including identifying stamps and documentation bearing the physician's signature. In 1804 the newly minted Dr. Samuel H. P. Lee of New London found himself in hot water with the Connecticut Medical Society. The Society objected to his advertising his New London pills "as an invaluable medicine, in almost every disease incident to mankind, and palming the same upon the public under the patronage of the Connecticut Medical Society." This last phrase likely was a reference to the fact that Dr. H. P. Lee had been including the fact that he was a "Member of the Connecticut Medical Society" in his advertisements.

However, the Society's concern seemed to be less about the appropriateness of the New London physician's promotion of his pills and more about allowing Connecticut doctors to benefit from his invention. He avoided being expelled from the Society by agreeing to reveal the recipe and allowing any member of the Society to make the pills and use them without fear of being charged with infringing on the New London physician's patent.

The recipe for New London bilious pills was in fact different from that for the Windham pills. One of its eight ingredients was mercury, which accounted for nearly 15 percent of the pills' makeup.

When the Connecticut Medical Society saw the recipe, it issued a public statement that in its opinion "an indiscriminate use of said pills is not advisable—that in many of the cases in which they are recommended, they are inefficacious, and in others injurious." Given the pills' high mercury content, along with "some other very active ingredients," the Society recommended that they should be taken only under a doctor's supervision.

Despite the bitter feud between the two Lees, and the Connecticut Medical Society's cautions about the New London pills, the market was apparently large enough to accommodate both Windham and New London bilious pills. They were sold up and down the Atlantic coast and beyond the Mississippi River. Dr. Lee of Windham renewed his patent when its original fourteen-year period expired in 1810. Dr. Lee of New London did the same when his patent expired in 1813. Others tried to get in on the action, including a third Samuel Lee, who claimed to be a nephew of Dr. Samuel Lee of Windham.

The inventor of the "true & genuine" Windham bilious pills died in Windham in 1814, at the age of forty-one. The cause of his death, and whether it was something he tried to treat with his own invention, is unknown.

Despite Lee's death, America's first patented medicine would continue to be available for decades to come. Charles Lee, Dr. Samuel Lee's younger brother, had supervised the actual production of the pills while his brother was alive. With the help of others, he carried on the bilious pill business into the 1840s.

There is an odd side note to the subject of biliousness in the eighteenth and nineteenth centuries. A few parents bestowed the first name of Bilious on their children. Colonial families often gave their children names that reflected the virtues they should emulate, such as Charity, Hope, and Faith. But Bilious? One can only wonder.

1814

Turning 'Em Out Like Clockwork

They're everywhere—in our bedrooms, our cars, our kitchens, our offices, our bathrooms, our classrooms. They regulate just about every aspect of our lives to a degree that sometimes seems tyrannical. They are clocks, and the man who deserves the credit—or the curses—for making their "tick-tock" the rhythm of daily life for the average American is Eli Terry of Connecticut.

The ability to always know the exact time to the hour and minute and to structure most of our lives around that knowledge is a relatively new phenomenon in human history. Up until the early 1800s—just two centuries ago—people told time primarily by consulting nature. A meeting might be set to start at "candle-light"—when it was dark enough to require lighting candles to see—not exact, but precise enough that people would arrive more or less on time. The Sabbath day was over when four stars could be seen together in a single glance at the Sunday night sky. People who needed to know the time more precisely could use devices such as sundials or hourglasses, or they could consult the almanac found in just about every American home for the exact times of sunrise and sunset and coordinate the time with the event.

These methods sufficed for most folk, who rarely needed to know the exact time. The vast majority of Americans were farmers whose days and nights were structured by what tasks needed to be done, how much daylight would be available, and the changing seasons.

This was just as well, for during the 1700s a clock was an extravagance beyond the budget of all but the wealthy. Each clock—its mechanism, its dial, its case—had to be made entirely by hand by one or more craftsmen who had trained for years. It required months to assemble a single clock, usually for a customer who had ordered one. In Connecticut clocks were so universally understood to be symbols of affluence that their owners paid a tax on them—not a sales tax levied on the price at the time of purchase, but a property tax that had to be paid every year.

Eli Terry, who would make it possible for every house, no matter how humble, to possess a clock, was born in 1772 in South Windsor, Connecticut. He served a seven-year apprenticeship with a master clock maker to learn how to fashion the works and the dial for the only kind of clock then made, a tall clock with weights and a pendulum—what today would be called a grandfather clock.

When Terry turned twenty-one, he moved to the town of Plymouth in western Connecticut. For a time he continued to pursue his craft in the traditional ways, making the works (sometimes fashioned out of wood, sometimes out of brass) and the dial for one or two clocks at a time. It was up to the customer to arrange for a joiner to make a wooden case to house Terry's mechanism. Some people, unable or unwilling to pay for a case, simply hung the mechanism on the wall.

For a few years Terry also worked as a peddler, traveling as far as Kentucky, carrying with him the mechanisms for perhaps four clocks. Priced at twenty-five dollars apiece, he found them a hard sell.

But Eli Terry belonged to the post–Revolutionary War generation of Connecticut, which produced an extraordinary number of individuals with the passion and the genius for coming up with new and better ways of doing things. Around 1800 Terry began to experiment with using waterpower to run some of his clock-making equipment and with making some of the parts interchangeable. His goal was to produce clocks faster and more cheaply.

By 1805 Terry had begun work on two hundred clocks simultaneously. That ambitious move earned him the mockery and pity of his neighbors, who predicted that the thirty-three-year-old Terry wouldn't live long enough to finish them all. If by some miracle he did complete them, he would never be able to sell them all, his critics agreed. Terry ignored the doubters, and within two years he was turning out about two hundred clocks annually in what has been called the first clock factory in America.

Terry put his new water-powered, interchangeable-parts system of manufacturing to the acid test in 1806 when he signed a contract to deliver four thousand wooden tall-clock mechanisms in three years. Not surprisingly, his contemporaries again laughed at him. The laugh was on them when

Terry fulfilled the contract on time, at a cut-rate cost of four dollars for each mechanism.

Terry had proved that he could make clocks faster than anyone thought possible, and at a lower cost—and in doing so he had made enough money to live on for the rest of his life. Having significantly improved the process of making clocks, he now turned his ingenuity to improving the product itself. After two years of work, he perfected the timepiece that would make it possible for just about anyone, anywhere to own a clock.

This revolutionary invention was the wooden shelf clock—so called for the simple reason that the mechanism, dial, weight, and pendulum were all contained in a case about two feet tall and four or five inches deep; thus the clock was short enough and light enough to stand on a shelf. The clock would run for thirty hours before it needed rewinding.

The shelf clock's compact size meant that peddlers could carry more of them on their selling trips. The fact that they came complete with the case made them a more salable product. Shelf clocks were much less expensive to make, and of course Terry could apply the technology that had enabled him to successfully fill his contract for four thousand tall-clock mechanisms to turning out shelf clocks in large numbers. By 1819 the Terry family enterprise in Plymouth, which now included two of the inventor's sons, was turning out six thousand shelf clocks, complete with wooden case, each year, at a cost of fifteen dollars each.

Adding to the shelf clock's appeal was its attractive appearance. Early on, the cases of Terry's shelf clocks were made in a "pillar and scroll" design—with wooden pillars flanking the clock face, a scroll pediment or top, and often finished off with brass finials. The faces of the clocks were painted by hand, and below the clock face itself many also featured a glass window on which a decorative scene was painted.

Peddlers were the main marketers and distributors of shelf clocks. They sold them by the tens of thousands throughout the United States east of the Mississippi River.

Other men knew a good thing when they saw it, and more clock factories sprang up in and around the town of Plymouth to duplicate or capitalize on Terry's success. By 1836 Bristol boasted sixteen clock factories, which turned out one hundred thousand clocks annually—at a time when the population of the United States was barely thirteen million.

Terry himself had already retired, in 1833, letting his sons run the clock empire he had established. New entrepreneurs and new ideas kept the clock industry in Connecticut flourishing.

By the outbreak of the Civil War, Connecticut was producing half a million clocks a year. In a country of thirty-one million people, that was enough to put a clock in every household in a few short years. Thanks to the imagination and entrepreneurship of Eli Terry, America and the world were—for better or worse—well on their way to an existence structured by the hands of a clock.

1817

Breaking the
Soundless Barrier

Thomas Hopkins Gallaudet, an ordained minister with degrees from Yale and Andover Theological Seminary who had worked at occupations ranging from preaching to peddling, was a young man in search of a mission. At twenty-six years old, he had yet to discover his calling in life.

Fate solved Gallaudet's dilemma on a June day in 1814, in the front yard of his parents' Hartford home, where he met a little deaf girl named Alice Cogswell. That serendipitous encounter would lead to the establishment of the first school for the deaf in the United States.

Alice Cogswell was the nine-year-old daughter of Dr. Mason Fitch Cogswell, an eminent surgeon and president of the Connecticut Medical Society. When Alice was two, a fever, possibly meningitis, rendered her deaf. Her inability to hear meant that as Alice grew up, she also didn't learn to speak.

In the early 1800s in the United States, deaf people and their loved ones had nowhere to turn for help. No treatment for hearing loss and no schools to address the special communication and learning needs of deaf people were available. This state of affairs was aggravated by the prevailing belief that a deaf person must also be of limited intelligence.

Alice's physician father was determined to do whatever he could to help the child. He discovered that there were schools for the deaf in England and France. From the latter, he ordered books that he hoped would provide some guidance, including one about a system of sign language.

Despite Dr. Cogswell's energetic attempts, he was unable to bridge the chasm of silence between Alice and the rest of the world. Capable of only the most fundamental communication with gestures and facial expressions, unable to read or write and thus denied any education, Alice seemed doomed to a life of lonely, dependent isolation.

Then came that fateful June day, when Thomas Gallaudet sat on the porch of his parents' house, idly watching a gaggle of children that included some of his own eight younger siblings playing a boisterous game of tag.

After a while Gallaudet realized that one little girl was not participating in the play. Instead she stood by herself, apart, watching the other children. Gallaudet's brother Teddy explained: the girl was Alice Cogswell, nine years old, the same as Teddy, and she couldn't hear or talk.

Intrigued, Gallaudet, who had no teaching experience, approached the child. He spent the rest of the afternoon working with Alice, painstakingly and repeatedly tracing out the letters "H" "A" "T" in the dirt with a stick, and then pointing to his hat. At last Alice experienced a "eureka" moment of understanding that the marks in the dirt stood for the hat.

Dr. Cogswell arrived home in time to witness the near-miraculous breakthrough in helping his daughter. He gave Gallaudet the books he had acquired from France and asked the young man to become Alice's teacher. Gallaudet agreed and spent the next ten months, when he wasn't off preaching at churches around the region, teaching Alice both written words and the hand signs he had learned from the French books. Alice proved to be a quick student. She mastered the signs for as many as twenty words a day, developing the ability to speak with her hands.

Dr. Cogswell was so thrilled and encouraged by his daughter's progress that in April 1815 he arranged for Gallaudet and Alice to make a presentation before a gathering of influential Hartford leaders.

Dr. Cogswell then appealed to the group to raise enough money to send a man to Europe to study the state-of-the-art methods for educating the deaf and bring that knowledge back to the United States. The undertaking would not be intended to benefit Alice Cogswell alone. After his daughter lost her hearing, Dr. Cogswell had conducted a survey that indicated there were dozens of deaf children in Connecticut and hundreds across the country. Any surplus funds collected would be applied to establishing a school for the deaf in Hartford—the first in the nation.

The fund-raising exceeded anyone's expectations. In a single day the enormous sum of $2,133—the equivalent of more than $39,000 in 2022 dollars—was collected, in a city of only six thousand residents. The logical—the only—candidate for the mission was Thomas Hopkins Gallaudet. He sailed for Europe on May 25, 1815.

Gallaudet went first to England, where instruction of the deaf was monopolized by members of the Braidwood family, who considered their methods a trade secret to be exploited for as much money as possible. They were willing to share their knowledge with Gallaudet only if he agreed to sign on for a minimum of three years as a kind of apprentice. It was an unacceptable option for Gallaudet, who had only a year to learn as much as he could in Europe.

Once again serendipity saved the day. The Abbé Sicard, author of the books Dr. Cogswell had imported years earlier in his desperate effort to help Alice, happened to be in London (having departed Paris to avoid Napoleon Bonaparte's brief attempt at regaining control of France). Gallaudet attended a demonstration by Sicard, at which he encountered living proof of the success of the method of instruction offered at Sicard's Institut National des Jeunes Sourds-Muets (National Institute for Young Deaf-Mutes) in the person of Laurent Clerc, a former student and now a teacher at the Institut National.

When Gallaudet explained his mission to the Abbé Sicard, the response he received was the exact opposite of that of the Braidwoods. Gallaudet was invited to come to Paris and learn everything about teaching the deaf that the Institut National had to offer.

Gallaudet spent more than six months familiarizing himself with the French courses of instruction for the deaf. In August 1816 he arrived back in the United States, accompanied by Laurent Clerc, who had agreed to become a teacher at the proposed new school for the deaf.

But first the money to start up the school had to be raised. Like many a school head and professor before and since, Gallaudet and Clerc embarked on expeditions throughout New England to raise as much as possible of the more than $15,000—more than $275,000 in 2022 dollars—required.

In 1816 the Connecticut General Assembly granted the proposed school $5,000. That funding, combined with the private donations, constituted a sufficient sum to establish in Hartford the Connecticut Asylum for the Education and Instruction of Deaf and Dumb Persons. It opened on April 14, 1817, with Thomas Gallaudet as principal, Laurent Clerc as instructor, and Alice Cogswell as the first student. Before the year was over, the student body had grown to 33. A year later it had quadrupled, to 125.

In 1821 the school built a brand-new four-story building on land on Asylum Avenue—which got its name from the school. The new facility had been made possible in part by a grant from the U.S. Congress of twenty-three thousand acres of wilderness land in Alabama. The land was sold, and the proceeds were used to finance the new school, which stood for a century.

On December 10, 1830, Dr. Mason Cogswell died of pneumonia in the arms of his daughter Alice, then twenty-five. The agony of the loss was intensified by fear of how Alice would react, now that she was bereft of the father who had been her champion and her friend.

Before the clock struck midnight, those fears proved justified. Alice dissolved into violent hysterics; when exhaustion finally stilled her, she signed to Gallaudet, "Father's dead. I die, too." Her father's passing had broken something in the young woman's spirit that no amount of reassurance or loving attention by family or friends could fix. Alice refused to eat, and on December 23 she, too, died.

The year 1830 also brought another ending for Thomas Gallaudet: his retirement as principal of the school for the deaf. Nonetheless, he continued to work, writing children's books that sold millions of copies internationally, in part because he needed to support his wife, Sophia, who had been one of the school's first students, and their family. Eventually their family would number eight children, including a daughter born in 1833 who was named Alice Cogswell Gallaudet.

In 1850 friends and the board of directors of the school for the deaf presented Gallaudet with sufficient funds to buy a house not far from the school. He died the following year.

But Thomas Gallaudet's service to the deaf community was not yet complete. His youngest child, Edward Miner Gallaudet, set out to fulfill his father's dream of deaf people having the opportunity to pursue what today would be considered a high school education, or even to attend college. In 1857 Edward was instrumental in establishing in Washington, D.C. what today is Gallaudet University, the world's only institution of higher education dedicated to education of the deaf.

Back in Connecticut, Gallaudet's legacy endures. In 1921 the school he helped found moved to West Hartford, where today it operates as the American School for the Deaf.

The little girl who was the catalyst for the movement for education of the deaf in America is commemorated by a statue across from the site on Asylum Avenue in Hartford where the nation's first school for the deaf stood for a century and where the Hartford Insurance Company is located today. Situated on the Y formed by the intersection of Farmington and Asylum avenues, it depicts Alice Cogswell standing tall, clutching a book to her chest, supported by hands making the sign for "light." The figure symbolizes all of the deaf children in the United States who have benefited from the educational opportunities made possible by the revolutionary accomplishments of the American School for the Deaf.

1839

Burning Rubber

"Obsession" doesn't begin to adequately describe Charles Goodyear's pursuit of the secret to rubber. The Connecticut native spent five years conducting countless experiments to discover how to stabilize rubber so that it could be fashioned into an array of waterproof goods. Once he cracked the mystery, he devoted another five years to perfecting the process before patenting it. The remainder of his life—fifteen years—he passed in an ultimately unsuccessful effort to profit from his discovery.

Goodyear was born in New Haven on December 29, 1800, at the very dawn of the century that would see the United States, and Connecticut in particular, develop into a powerhouse of technological innovation and manufacturing. While Charles was still a child, the family moved to

Naugatuck, where his father farmed and also owned a small water-powered mill that made ivory buttons.

When he was just sixteen, Charles moved to Philadelphia to work for five years in a hardware store. Returning to Connecticut, he joined his father's firm, which had branched out into making farm tools. By 1826 Goodyear, now married, was back in Philadelphia, running his own hardware store. His stock included farm implements turned out by the family firm in Naugatuck.

The Goodyear family's financial future looked rosy. But then Charles was sidelined by illness, and a national economic downturn made it impossible to collect money owed to him. The Goodyear store went out of business, and Charles was hounded by his own creditors and eventually spent some time in debtor's prison. Two of Goodyear's children died before reaching the age of four.

It was in 1834, during this period of financial and personal crisis, that Charles Goodyear first began to think seriously about the intriguing substance called gum elastic or India rubber. Made from a fluid obtained from trees grown in Brazil, it possessed remarkable properties: it was waterproof, elastic, and malleable. Ideas for the many different products that could be made from it tantalized inventors and merchants. A few entrepreneurs had actually fashioned goods such as life preservers out of rubber.

But—and this was a huge "but"—raw rubber had other properties that rendered it unusable for just about any application. When it's warm, rubber is sticky and doesn't hold its shape. When it's cold, rubber turns brittle and easily breaks. It emits an unpleasant odor and, given enough time, will rot.

Charles Goodyear realized that whoever could unlock the secret of making rubber usable could expect to be rewarded with fame and fortune. Goodyear became besotted with rubber like another man might be with alcohol or women or power.

Goodyear devoted every dime he had and every waking minute to his rubber experiments. The methods of experimentation available to him and others chasing the same dream were barely a step above trial and error. Goodyear often conducted his tests in his family's kitchen.

Goodyear tried all manner of treatment and additives, including magnesia, lampblack, turpentine, quicklime, nitric acid, and lead oxide, among many others. Again and again it would appear that the critical breakthrough had been made. Goods such as shoes, rubber-lined fabric, and mailbags would be produced from the treated rubber in factories in which Goodyear held an interest, and the Goodyear family's financial picture would brighten. Inevitably, though, after the passage of a few months, the goods would display one of rubber's undesirable qualities—they would start to decompose or become sticky.

Goodyear's monomania meant that he rarely held a steady, paying job, for regular employment would interfere with his research. He ran through backers, partners, and investors in his manic quest, borrowing from so many creditors that even he couldn't keep track of what he owed. He was in and out of debtor's prison.

As a result of his fixation on rubber to the exclusion of all else, Goodyear's wife and children were shuttled between New York and Philadelphia and Boston and New Haven, depending on where Goodyear happened to be seeking financing or conducting experiments. One time Goodyear sold the household furniture, another time his children's schoolbooks, to raise money to continue his experiments.

The family's situation grew so desperate that at one point they were reduced to catching frogs and digging half-frozen potatoes in order to have something—anything—to quiet the pangs of hunger. Two sons died while still toddlers, their deaths very likely hastened by the grim impact of poverty. Still, Goodyear's wife and children stood by him.

The "lightbulb" moment for Charles Goodyear arrived on a winter's day in early 1839. During a stay in Woburn, Massachusetts, Goodyear wrote years later, he "made some experiments to ascertain the effect of heat upon" rubber into which he had mixed sulfur and white lead. The results were promising, but then, as had happened so many times before, the rubber began to decompose.

However, Goodyear recalled, he "was surprised to find that the specimens being carelessly brought into contact with a hot stove, charred like leather"—which was the effect he had been seeking. Serendipity had achieved what years of relentless experimentation had not.

By using the word "carelessly," Goodyear acknowledged that chance had played a part in his discovery that applying heat of a certain temperature and for a certain period of time was the key. Nonetheless, he wrote, in words that he italicized, he "was not willing to admit that they were the result of what is commonly termed accident."

Goodyear compared himself to Sir Isaac Newton divining the existence of gravity from observing the simple act of an apple falling from a tree. The effect on the rubber of being "carelessly brought into contact with a hot stove," Goodyear claimed, "was suggestive of an important fact to one whose mind was previously prepared to draw an inference from any occurrence which might favor the object of his research." In other words, Goodyear, with his years of experience studying and experimenting with rubber, was able to perceive the significance of what others less steeped in rubber research saw only as a small, unimportant accident.

Goodyear, a deeply religious man, also credited God with a role in the discovery: "It may, therefore, be considered as one of those cases where the leading of the Creator providentially aids his creatures, by what are termed 'accidents,' to attain those things which are not attainable by the powers of reasoning he has conferred on them."

Mixing sulfur and white lead with rubber, then heating it at the correct temperature for a specified length of time—a process that a British competitor would soon dub "vulcanization," after Vulcan, the Roman god of fire and craftsmanship—solved all of rubber's drawbacks. Goodyear spent another five years of sacrifice, tedium, and financial hardship before he had improved the process sufficiently that he felt confident seeking a patent from the U.S. government. In the meantime, he was the target of industrial espionage and unscrupulous competitors.

The U.S. patent on vulcanization was granted to Goodyear on June 15, 1844. Several mills had already been set up in Massachusetts and in Naugatuck to make goods out of vulcanized rubber. Goodyear began to earn enough money to lift his family out of poverty, but the inventor was still so burdened with debt that he couldn't raise the funds to capitalize significantly on his patent.

Goodyear soon became hopelessly snarled in a tangle of legal disputes about patents and licensing that quickly spanned the Atlantic. He spent most of the 1850s in Europe promoting and patenting and litigating about his vulcanized rubber.

Goodyear returned to the United States in 1858 and took up residence in Washington, D.C. In June 1860 he received word that one of his grown daughters was gravely ill in New Haven. He headed immediately for Connecticut. Upon reaching New York, he learned that the daughter had died. Goodyear, who suffered from poor health periodically for decades, partly induced by the hazardous materials he used in his experiments, collapsed and died on July 1, 1860.

Charles Goodyear was buried in Grove Street Cemetery in New Haven, the city of his birth. He was more than $200,000 in debt when he died—easily the equivalent of $6 million and probably much more in 2022 dollars.

Although Goodyear's actual discovery of vulcanization didn't happen in Connecticut, some of his experiments did, and his roots in Naugatuck were responsible for the birth of the state's rubber industry. In 1843 Goodyear's daughter Ellen showed the process of making overshoes from vulcanized rubber to her uncle and three other entrepreneurs in Naugatuck. One of the entrepreneurs, Samuel Lewis, converted his Naugatuck knitting mill into one producing overshoes made of vulcanized rubber, under the first license granted by Charles Goodyear.

Before another five years passed, four more companies in Naugatuck were making shoes under Goodyear licenses. From those fledgling factories grew the rubber industry that would define and dominate Naugatuck for nearly 150 years, employing thousands of workers in mills turning out rubber products that were marketed around the globe.

Today the name Goodyear is familiar to most people from the Goodyear Tire & Rubber Company and especially from the Goodyear blimp, which provides aerial television coverage of sports events across the country and internationally.

But in fact the company has no connection to Charles Goodyear. The men who established it in Akron, Ohio, in 1898, chose the name because of the enduring connection in the public mind between Goodyear and rubber.

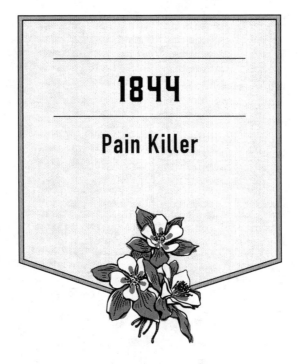

1844

Pain Killer

On a December night in 1844, Hartford dentist Horace Wells and his wife went to Union Hall for a night of light entertainment. What Wells got was an inspiration that would lead to one of the greatest medical blessings in the history of humankind—and to tragedy for Wells himself.

Wells, just twenty-eight, had operated a flourishing dental practice in Hartford since 1836. Married with a young son, he was generally regarded as "an upright and estimable man."

When trying to treat their patients, dentists of that era labored under an enormous handicap: the lack of anesthesia. Teeth had to be cleaned, treated for decay, and extracted while the patient was completely awake, and there were no injectable anesthetics such as Novocain to numb the pain.

A trip to the dentist often was a desperate last resort, when the agony and/or inconvenience of a cavity or some other problem became greater than the fear of the pain the dentist would unavoidably inflict.

That was the stressful reality of Horace Wells's professional life until that fateful night in 1844, when he attended a demonstration by Gardner Quincy Colton of the amusingly animating effects produced by inhaling nitrous oxide, also known as laughing gas. Audience members were invited to participate, and one man of Wells's acquaintance, Samuel Cooley, raced around the room while under the influence. He finally resumed his seat near Wells, who noticed that during his energetic antics Cooley had received a nasty gash in his leg. When Wells called Cooley's attention to the bloody injury, Cooley was surprised, saying that he hadn't noticed receiving it and that he felt no pain.

Wells immediately grasped the potential benefits of such a pain blocker. He decided to test his idea the very next day, with himself as the human guinea pig. He would have a decayed molar extracted while under the influence of nitrous oxide.

The following morning Colton administered laughing gas to Wells in the dentist's office on Main Street. According to Wells, he directed his partner, Dr. J. M. Riggs, "to perform the operation at the moment when I should give the signal, resolving to have the tooth extracted before losing all consciousness. This experiment proved to be perfectly successful—it was attended with no pain whatever."

Over the next month Wells used nitrous oxide to successfully sedate more than a dozen patients while treating them. "Elated with this discovery," he headed for Boston, home of the prestigious Harvard Medical School and Massachusetts

General Hospital. There Wells looked up William Morton, who had been his dental student and later his partner. Wells and Morton approached John Warren, a professor of surgery at the hospital, with an offer for Wells to demonstrate the power of nitrous oxide for medicinal purposes.

Arrangements were made for Wells to administer nitrous oxide to a patient scheduled to have an arm removed on January 20, 1845. Although amputating a limb was considerably more complicated than pulling a tooth, Wells agreed, only to have the patient back out.

From the group of physicians and medical students gathered to observe the demonstration, a student volunteered to allow Wells to administer nitrous oxide to him and then pull a tooth.

The equipment Wells used to administer the nitrous oxide looked more like something out of a medieval torture chamber than a medical supply catalog. It consisted of an animal's bladder to contain the gas and a wooden spout that was placed between the patient's lips. With the patient's nostrils pinched together, the bladder was compressed, expelling the nitrous oxide into the patient's mouth.

In his Boston demonstration, Wells, who had been administering anesthesia for little more than a month, made the mistake of not keeping the pipe inserted in the patient's mouth long enough to be sure he had inhaled enough gas to anesthetize him completely.

The tooth extraction went off without incident, but the patient afterward revealed that he had experienced some pain, although not as much as that normally associated with having a tooth pulled.

The eminent physicians present quickly dismissed nitrous oxide as a humbug. Humiliated but not discouraged,

Wells returned to Hartford, where he continued to use nitrous oxide to alleviate the pain of surgery.

Back in Boston, Wells's old partner William Morton, after consulting with another physician, Charles Jackson, decided to copy Wells's procedure using ether instead of nitrous oxide. In October 1846 the *Boston Daily Journal* ran a sworn statement from a patient who said he had been given ether by Morton and then had a tooth pulled painlessly. A couple of weeks later, physicians in Boston were treated to a demonstration in which Jackson removed a tumor painlessly from the neck of a patient whom Morton had anesthetized with ether.

Morton and Jackson were claiming the glory of having "discovered" inhaled anesthesia. Morton sought a patent for the concept that Wells had intended to be a gift to all mankind.

Wells published a lengthy defense of his right to the title of discoverer of anesthesia in the *Hartford Daily Courant* on December 9, 1846. Shortly afterward he sailed to Europe.

In Paris Wells was delighted to learn that his work with anesthesia was known. He demonstrated the effectiveness of laughing gas at several major hospitals.

Upon returning to the United States, Wells once again took up his fight for recognition in his own country. In 1847 he published *History of the Discovery of the Application of Nitrous Oxide, Ether and Other Vapors in Surgical Operations*, making the case for his getting the credit.

Wells returned to practicing dentistry, opening an office in New York City, and began investigating the use of another substance, chloroform, for anesthetizing patients. It was there in January 1848 that he encountered the dark side of inhaled anesthesia.

During the third week of January, Wells had, in his own words, "been in the constant practice of inhaling chloroform for the exhilarating effect produced by it." On the night of Friday, January 21— Wells's thirty-third birthday—a scandalous incident occurred. Although many of the details were contradictory, Wells acknowledged the critical specifics.

On that Friday Wells had been inhaling chloroform. As he confessed, "I had lost all consciousness before I removed the inhaler from my mouth. How long it remained there I do not know, but on coming out of the stupor I was exhilarated beyond measure exceeding anything which I had ever before experienced." Upon arising, Wells noticed a vial of sulfuric acid on the mantel in his office. "In my delirium I seized it and rushed in the street and threw it at two females. I may have thrust it at others, but I have no recollection farther than this," Wells admitted.

The women whom Wells had splashed with acid were prostitutes. Wells claimed that the idea of the assault had been planted in his chloroform-addled brain by a young man who two nights earlier had asked Wells for some sulfuric acid to toss on the clothing of a prostitute who had "spoiled a garment for him while walking in the street, by throwing something like vitriol upon him." Wells had accompanied the man on his mission of retaliation that first night. The following evening, against Wells's advice, the man reportedly had recruited several friends to go out with him to toss acid at streetwalkers.

Wells, under suspicion not just for the Friday night incident but for the two earlier acid-throwing episodes as well, was arrested. He was held for trial without bail in the notorious Tombs jail.

"The effect of this inhalation continued very much longer than ever before," Wells recalled, "and did not entirely pass off until sometime after my arrest." Once his head cleared, Wells penned a letter to the *New York Journal of Commerce* newspaper explaining the situation, accepting responsibility for his actions of that Friday night, and vehemently denying his involvement in the earlier acid-throwing incidents.

> I state unhesitatingly that I would no sooner deliberately in cold blood, go into the street and commit the gross acts of wantonness that have been committed for the last few evenings, than I would cut my right hand from my body. . . . I am obliged to bear the reproaches of the world for the most contemptible acts in which I have not participated; because I have done this one act in a moment of delirium I must bear the brunt of the whole.

"My character, which I have ever prized above everything else is gone—irrevocably gone," Wells lamented. "I am now in the most miserable condition in which it is possible for man to be placed."

With the effects of the chloroform having worn off, Wells resumed being the cooperative, well-bred young man that he was. "The officer who had me in care kindly permitted me to go to my room yesterday," he wrote. There Wells picked up a bottle of chloroform and a razor that he took back to his cell.

At seven o'clock on Sunday night, Wells sat down in his cell and wrote a suicide note to his family. His greatest anguish was for his wife and son, "whom I leave destitute of the means of support—I would still live and work for you, but I cannot—for were I to live on I should became a maniac. I feel that I am but little better than one already."

"I die tonight, believing that God who knoweth all hearts will forgive the dreadful act. I shall spend my remaining time in prayer," Wells wrote. "Oh! what misery I shall bring upon all my near relations—and what still distresses me is the fact that my name is familiar to the whole scientific world, as being connected with an important discovery, and now . . . I must bid all farewell."

Wells then picked up the razor and, under the influence of the pain-numbing chloroform, slashed the femoral artery in a leg. He bled to death in his cell.

News of Wells's horrific suicide shocked and saddened Hartford. "Having just been acknowledged as the discoverer of etherization in surgical operations, there was no one who seemed less likely to meet the sad fate that has befallen him."

Horace Wells's body was returned to Hartford for burial in Old North Cemetery. When the time came for his fellow medical professionals to evaluate his accomplishments, the tawdry crime committed under the influence of chloroform that he felt had fouled his reputation so badly that he could not go on living was considered insignificant. In 1864 the American Dental Association acknowledged Wells as the discoverer of modern anesthesia, and the American Medical Association accorded him the same honor in 1870, and again in 1944.

In 1908, sixty years after Wells's death, his son had his parents' bodies moved from Old North Cemetery to Cedar Hill Cemetery, the lavishly landscaped burial ground that is the final resting place of Hartford luminaries such as Sam Colt and J. P. Morgan. To mark their graves, he commissioned an ornate monument that dramatically displays to the world the relief of pain that was Horace Wells's great gift to humanity.

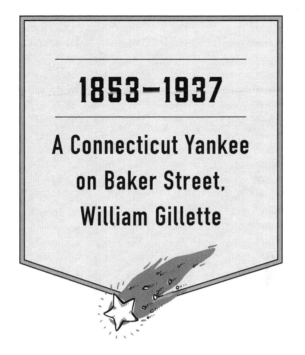

1853–1937

A Connecticut Yankee on Baker Street, William Gillette

British author Sir Arthur Conan Doyle created "consulting detective" Sherlock Holmes on the pages of four novels and fifty-six short stories in the late nineteenth and early twentieth centuries. But Conan Doyle's eccentric, brilliant sleuth was first brought to flesh-and-blood life by Connecticut's William Gillette, in a theatrical performance that more than 120 years later continues to influence how Holmes is portrayed in everything from television to film to radio to cartoons to video games.

William Gillette, the man who would become Sherlock Holmes, was born in 1853 in Nook Farm, a neighborhood of Hartford, Connecticut, that was home to luminaries of the intellectual and literary world. He was the son of U.S. Senator Francis Gillette and of Elizabeth Hooker, whose descent from Hartford founding father Reverend Thomas Hooker meant William Gillette belonged to what passed for Connecticut aristocracy.

By the time he was a teenager, Gillette had developed a yearning to be an actor. It was a less-than-reputable line of work, especially for a young man of Gillette's class.

Gillette's father, not surprisingly, disapproved of the stage as a career for his son. However, the elder Gillette didn't stand in the way of William's ambition when at age twenty he embarked on the only way to secure training as an actor, there yet being no drama schools. For seven years Gillette took part in what amounted to an informal apprenticeship, playing roles in theatrical companies that toured the nation, staging several different plays during a stay in a particular city.

In 1880 Gillette began writing his own plays, both comedies and dramas. In addition to being a talented playwright, he also proved to be a gifted actor and a creative stage manager. He was also blessed with the good looks of the ideal leading man: more than six feet tall, lean, and reserved, he had an abundance of curly dark hair and a handsome face with an aquiline nose, deep-set brooding eyes, and chiseled cleft chin. Over the next two decades he successfully starred in plays, both his own and those by other authors, in theaters across the country and in England.

The opportunity that would elevate Gillette from successful Victorian era stage star to an enduring influence on popular drama and culture came from across the Atlantic. Between 1887 and 1893 Sir Arthur Conan Doyle penned a series of stories about the cases undertaken by his fictional detective Sherlock Holmes that proved wildly popular. In 1893 Conan Doyle, feeling that his Holmes writings were impeding his attempts to compose more serious literature, killed off his genius sleuth. Public outrage and grief over the demise of the fictional detective was tremendous.

Just four years later, however, Conan Doyle resurrected Holmes for that most fundamental of reasons: money. He wrote a play featuring Holmes and his associate Dr. John Watson early in their careers as investigators.

Conan Doyle failed to generate any interest in his play in England. Charles Frohman, an internationally successful theater owner, producer, and promoter of new dramatic talent, who had known Gillette for more than two decades, read Conan Doyle's treatment. Frohman proposed that William Gillette, with a track record of successes as an actor and playwright, be approached about revising the manuscript.

Gillette agreed to undertake the project and began by reading everything Conan Doyle had written about Sherlock Holmes. With Conan Doyle's consent, Gillette threw out the original play and wrote an entirely new work. His script incorporated elements from several of Conan Doyle's works.

Conan Doyle initially had only one condition for Gillette's play. Holmes, as written by Conan Doyle, was a primarily intellectual, calculating man, with no inclination toward affairs of the heart. Thus he instructed Gillette that "there was to be no love business" in the stage version of Holmes.

As work on the script proceeded, however, Gillette telegraphed Conan Doyle, asking, "May I marry Holmes?" Conan Doyle, apparently by now trusting in Gillette's creative judgment, replied, "You may marry him, or murder or do what you like with him." Gillette didn't marry off Holmes, but at the very end of the play the detective does declare his love for a young woman, Alice Faulkner.

In his on-stage portrayal of Holmes, Gillette incorporated features that have become essential elements of any depiction of the great detective. Conan Doyle's Holmes smoked a pipe, which actually played a role in his analytical process, as when he referred to a particularly thorny dilemma as "a three-pipe problem," meaning it would require the time to smoke three pipes of tobacco to analyze. Conan Doyle described Holmes's pipe as being of clay with a straight stem. But when William Gillette appeared on stage as Holmes, the pipe had a stem that curved downward, moving the bowl below his chin. This was apparently to accommodate his needs as an actor. To smoke a pipe with a straight stem meant that his hand would obscure his mouth when he was speaking his lines.

Gillette's Holmes also wore a deerstalker cap—a cloth hat with short bills in both the front and the back. This specific cap wasn't included in any of Conan Doyle's Holmes writings. It was added to the detective's image by artist Sidney Paget in his illustrations for Sherlock Holmes's stories published in *The Strand* magazine beginning in 1891.

Perhaps the most recognizable and enduring of Gillette's contributions to Sherlock Holmes was in the fashioning of the famous line, "Elementary, my dear Watson." That exact phrase doesn't appear in any of Conan Doyle's writings. In the script of Gillette's play, when Dr. Watson demands how Holmes can know small details about his life and person, Holmes replies, "Elementary! The child's play of deduction!" In a rare surviving recording of a radio broadcast of Gillette performing the play when he was eighty-two, he spoke the line as "Elementary, my dear fellow! Elementary! The child's play of deduction!" In the first talking film production about the detective, *The Return of Sherlock Holmes*, the actor playing Holmes spoke the phrase as "Elementary, my dear Watson." In that form it has become one of the best-known expressions in English.

Gillette's own physical appearance, which resembled Conan Doyle's description of Holmes, became a defining quality of the detective. William Gillette "gave his face to" Sherlock Holmes, declared legendary actor and director Orson Welles in 1938. "William Gillette was the aquiline and actual embodiment of Holmes himself. It is too little to say that William Gillette resembled Sherlock Holmes; Sherlock Holmes looks exactly like William Gillette."

After a single private performance to establish copyright in England, and some out-of-town tryouts in cities in New York State and Pennsylvania, the four-act play *Sherlock Holmes*, staged by Charles Frohman, with Gillette in the title role, opened on Broadway on November 6, 1899. It was an instant hit with the public. It would run for 235 performances on Broadway, all sold out.

In 1901 Gillette took the play to Holmes's hometown of London, where it ran for more than 260 performances, all sold out as in New York. Conan Doyle himself was delighted with Gillette's interpretation of his creation. He wrote to Gillette, "my only complaint being that you make the poor hero of the anemic printed page a very limp object as compared with the glamour of your own personality which you infuse into his stage presentment."

Over the next three decades, Gillette would reprise the role of Sherlock Holmes more than 1,300 times across the United States and in England. It made him an international celebrity and a rich man.

Gillette last trod the boards as Sherlock Holmes in 1932, at nearly eighty years of age. He died five years later in 1937 in Hartford.

But William Gillette's spirit lives on in portrayals of Sherlock Holmes. Professor Russell Merritt, an expert on the famous fictional detective, stated, "As far as Holmes is concerned, there's not an actor dead or alive who hasn't consciously or intuitively played off Gillette." They number in the dozens, on television and in film alone, including Gillette himself. The better known include Basil Rathbone, John Cleese, Frank Langella, Roger Moore, Christopher Plummer, Peter O'Toole, Michael Caine, and Jeremy Brett. The popularity of Sherlock Holmes as envisioned by William Gillette continues unabated into the twenty-first century, as witnessed by portrayals by actors Robert Downey Jr., Johnny Lee Miller, Benedict Cumberbatch, Ian McKellan, and Will Ferrell.

Gillette also left a unique legacy for his native state. In 1914 he began a five-year project to build a "retirement home" on more than one hundred acres on a hill on the border of the towns of East Haddam and Lyme, Connecticut, with a magnificent view of the Connecticut River. Gillette himself designed the unique structure: a three-story, twenty-four-room building made primarily of rough Connecticut fieldstone that looks like a castle transplanted from medieval Europe.

Gillette also applied his ingenuity to designing the interior, which features an abundance of wood decoration and furniture, down to the light switches and complicated locks on the doors, as well as secret passageways and even a secret room. Guests to Gillette's extraordinary home, which he called Seventh Sister after the hill on which it was located, included Albert Einstein, President Calvin Coolidge, and stage and screen legends Helen Hayes and Charlie Chaplin.

Gillette had been married from 1882 to 1888, to Helen Nichols, a young woman he first spotted in the audience of one of his performances in Detroit. She died in 1888 of a ruptured appendix. The couple had no children, and Gillette never remarried.

As Gillette drafted his will in early 1937 (his estate would be valued at $113,000, worth more than $2 million today), he realized that of his few heirs none likely would want to take up residence in his cherished Seventh Sister, or Gillette Castle, as it was being called. This meant that the property would likely be sold. In his will he expressed his wish that his executors see that Seventh Sister not become the property of "some blithering sap-head who has no conception of where he is or with what surrounded."

Efforts to sell the property after Gillette's death brought in offers of less than half its estimated value. After six years, the estate was sold to the State of Connecticut, which in 1944 opened it as Gillette Castle State Park. Having undergone a multi-million-dollar restoration and renovation early in the twenty-first century, Gillette Castle, which is listed on the National Register of Historic Places, is visited by more than 350,000 people from around the globe each year.

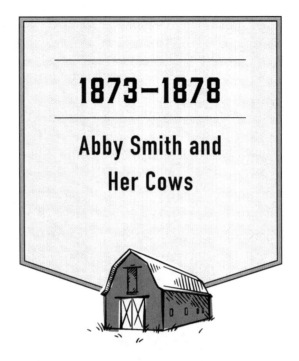

1873–1878

Abby Smith and Her Cows

The octogenarian spinster who in 1878 spoke before a committee of the U.S. Congress and urged members to grant women the right to vote wasn't merely "talking the talk." Julia Smith and her younger sister, Abby, had "walked the walk" by refusing to pay taxes to the town of Glastonbury, Connecticut, because they were not allowed to vote. Their stand for equal rights had catapulted the elderly duo to international prominence as symbols of the women's suffrage movement.

Less than ten years earlier, the Smith sisters were quietly living out their twilight years on the family homestead in Glastonbury. Even then they were by no means ordinary. Their father, Zephaniah, was a Yale-educated clergyman who left the ministry over religious differences to become a lawyer and farmer in Glastonbury. Their mother, Hannah Hadassah

Hickcock, had studied Latin, French, Italian, Greek, history, mathematics, and astronomy; wrote poetry; and in later life defied the law by helping fugitive slaves escape to freedom on the secret Underground Railroad.

Zephaniah and Hannah Smith had five daughters, of whom Julia, born in 1792, and Abby, born in 1797, were the youngest. Each had received an education more advanced than all but the most privileged men of their era, mastering history, literature, mathematics, and ancient and modern languages. Equally unusual for women of the 1800s, none of the Smith daughters married.

By 1872 only Julia, eighty, and Abby, seventy-five, were left in the big old house on their father's 130-acre farm. Given their family's unorthodox history, it wasn't surprising that the sisters took an interest in the women's suffrage movement, which had been brewing for several decades. In 1869 they had attended a suffrage meeting in Hartford that featured some of the giants of the crusade, including Elizabeth Cady Stanton and Susan B. Anthony. But Julia and Abby took action only after the injustice of women's disenfranchisement hit home for them—literally.

In 1872 the sisters learned that the value of their property had been revised upward by the town assessor, resulting in a small increase in their taxes. The additional tax was no financial burden to the sisters, who were among the wealthiest residents of Glastonbury.

But they were incensed when they discovered that only two other property owners in Glastonbury had had their property values increased—and both were women. They paid the tax, but the unfairness of it continued to rankle.

In the spring of 1873, Julia and Abby Smith attempted to register to vote in Glastonbury—only to be thwarted by a classic bureaucratic shuffle. When taxes came due that autumn, the sisters refused to pay, citing the same tyranny of "taxation without representation" that had spurred the Founding Fathers to rebel against Great Britain a century earlier.

The sisters took their case to the Glastonbury town meeting on November 5, 1873. Abby, the more outgoing of the two, did the speaking. She delivered a blistering critique in which she told the gathering of men that "the Southern slaveholder only possessed the same power that you have to rule over us." She also made an audacious assertion: "We cannot see why we are not just as capable of assisting in managing the affairs of the town as the men are."

Abby's radical comments were "scrupulously ignored" by the assembled citizenry, according to one report. But the Smith sisters shared something else with their Revolutionary forebears: an appreciation for the power of the press. Abby sent the text of her remarks at the Glastonbury town meeting to the *Hartford Courant* newspaper, which published them. The *Springfield Republican* newspaper in Massachusetts also quickly picked up on the story. Abby kept both journals apprised of the progress of their protest.

The sisters remained firm in their refusal to pay their taxes. On New Year's Day of 1874, the tax collector showed up at the Smith farm and confiscated seven Alderney cows to be sold at auction to cover the unpaid taxes. The dairy cows, a breed known for their gentleness, were more pets than livestock. The sisters had given them names such as Daisy, Bessie, and Minnie.

The situation now had the makings of a great human-interest story: plucky, independent, old maiden ladies standing up to defend one of the bedrock principles of democracy against the heartless tax collector who takes away their cherished pet cows. By the time the cows were auctioned on January 8, 1874, the story was getting play in Boston and Providence newspapers. The man who worked the Smith sisters' farm for them bought four of the cows at a price sufficient to cover the taxes and brought them back to the Smith farm. The town returned the three remaining Alderneys.

One tax bill had been settled, but the fundamental issue had not. At the suggestion of the *Springfield Republican* newspaper, the "Abby Smith Defense Fund" was established to receive contributions toward paying any legal bills the sisters might incur in their fight. In April, when Julia and Abby again sought to present their case before the Glastonbury town meeting, they were denied a chance to speak. A determined Abby mounted a wagon next to the town hall, which she used as an impromptu pulpit to say her piece to anyone willing to listen.

Not satisfied with simply speaking and writing, the sisters petitioned the Connecticut General Assembly in May 1874 for the right to vote. Abby spoke at length to the legislature's Committee on Female Suffrage, which several weeks later responded patronizingly that "Abby Smith and sister will be granted leave to withdraw their petition asking that equal rights be conferred upon them the same as is conferred upon other citizens of the state."

Glastonbury officials remained unmoved as well. The tax collector showed up as usual in April with the bill, and again Julia and Abby refused to pay it. This time the tax collector seized land, an action less likely to generate sympathetic publicity than had the confiscation of the sisters' pet cows.

However, since real estate could be seized for payment of taxes only in the absence of any "movable" possessions (of which Julia and Abby had an abundance, including, of course, their cows), the tax collector had violated the law. When the time came for the land to be auctioned, the sisters discovered that corruption also was afoot.

The tax collector had made a deal to sell eleven acres that just happened to be the best land on the Smith farm to a neighbor who had coveted them for years. For $78.35, the amount of the unpaid tax bill, the neighbor acquired land worth $2,000. Julia and Abby took the tax collector and their greedy neighbor to court and won their case after a two-year battle.

Glastonbury officials went back to seizing personal property to pay for the sisters' taxes. They auctioned off bank stock the sisters owned, while the unfortunate Alderneys were seized, auctioned, and bought back by Julia and Abby not once but twice in 1876. Finally, having taken a drubbing in the national press, Glastonbury simply gave up trying to make the sisters pay their taxes.

The sisters' stand for equality resonated with a nation exuberantly celebrating the centennial of the American Revolution. Julia and Abby had become celebrities and frequently spoke at women's suffrage gatherings. Their story was reported in publications from California to Connecticut and even in Europe.

In 1877 Julia published a selection from the hundreds of articles about their struggle that had appeared in newspapers in cities such as New York, Chicago, Washington, D.C., and Baltimore. Titled *Abby Smith and Her Cows*, it was illustrated with an engraving of Abby and the pet Alderneys.

The following January Julia and Abby Smith attended the National Woman Suffrage Association's convention in Washington, D.C. Julia, then eighty-five, addressed the

Congressional Committee on Privileges and Elections in Washington. "This is the first time in my life that I have trod these halls, and what has brought me here?" she told the legislators tartly. "I say oppression—oppression of women by men."

That speech was the final highlight in the Smith sisters' crusade for equality and justice. Abby died in July 1878 at the age of eighty-one, leaving Julia bereft of family for the first time in her long life.

Less than a year later, Julia astonished everyone by taking a husband at the age of eighty-seven. She married Amos Parker of New Hampshire, a widower twice over whose first contact with her had been a note of condolence on Abby's death.

From the town's perspective the marriage was a welcome development because Parker, as Julia's husband, paid taxes on the property, although it was reported that Julia later reimbursed him. As a personal union it was apparently less satisfactory. Some people suspected Parker was most interested in Julia's money, and he also proved to be somewhat overbearing. In 1884 the farm and house that had been in the Smith family for nearly a century, along with most of the household furnishings, were sold. Julia left the only home she had ever known to spend her last years with her husband in Newington and then Hartford, where she died in 1886, at the age of ninety-three.

Julia proved every bit as unconventional and independent in death as she had been in life. At her written direction, she was laid to rest with her four sisters and parents in a grave marked by a stone that gives no hint of her marriage but reads simply "Julia E. Smith."

The cows "are again complacently chewing their cuds in Abby Smith's comfortable barn," observed the *Boston*

Herald following the first auction in January 1874. "But the case has given a tough cud to the country to chew upon until the new Declaration of Independence is achieved and Abby Smith votes."

Abby Smith never did vote, nor did Julia. But victory in the fight they had championed did come nearly half a century after they had taken their stand. In 1920 the Nineteenth Amendment to the Constitution, which grants women the right to vote, was ratified. Today the Smith house in Glastonbury is a National Historic Landmark.

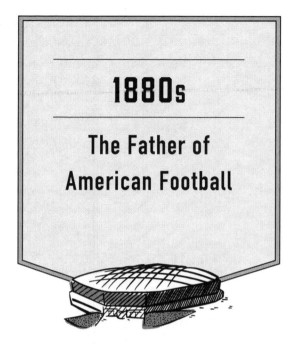

1880s

The Father of American Football

Millions of gridiron fans have Connecticut's Walter Camp to thank for some of the fundamentals of the game they love, including the eleven-man teams facing off at the line of scrimmage, the snap to the quarterback, and the system of downs and yards to go. In just four years between 1880 and 1884, Camp, not yet thirty years old, revised the English game of rugby into a separate, unique sport, earning him enduring renown as "the Father of American Football."

Walter Chauncey Camp was born in Connecticut in 1859. He attended the Hopkins Grammar School in New Haven and then enrolled in Yale in 1876. At Yale, Camp played on the varsity teams of every sport, including baseball, swimming, tennis, crew, and the brand-new addition to the roster, rugby.

Rugby, an English game, was just gaining popularity on the campuses of American colleges. In rugby as it was then played, teams of fifteen men each pursued the object of the game: kicking the ball through the opponent's goalpost, similar to a modern football upright. The ball could be moved by kicking, dribbling, carrying, or throwing, but kicking was the only way to score. Sometimes there were disagreements on how to interpret the rules.

Walter Camp made the Yale rugby team as a freshman. Before the Yale-Harvard game that year, the Harvard captain reportedly mocked Camp's featherweight physique, demanding of the Yale captain, "You don't mean to let that child play, do you? He is too light. He will get hurt." The Yale captain replied, "He is young but he is all spirit and whipcord."

After receiving his bachelor's degree in 1880, Camp entered Yale Medical School. Prevailing regulations allowed him to continue playing on the Yale rugby team while he was studying medicine. He also began serving as Yale's first football coach, a volunteer position.

Like his ingenious fellow Connecticut Yankees, who were revolutionizing everything from manufacturing to marketing, Camp had many ideas about how to improve the game of rugby. While he was still in his teens, he put forth his first proposal: reduce the number of players on each team from fifteen to eleven. Cutting the total number of men on the field by more than one-quarter would make play less like mob action. It was formally adopted as a rule in 1880 by the Intercollegiate Football Association.

That same year saw the adoption of another of Camp's innovations that is fundamental to the modern structure of the game of football: the scrimmage. In rugby, when play needed to be restarted, it was done by means of a "scrum." In a scrum, eight players from each team arranged themselves in a three-line formation, with their arms around the waist of the players to their side and their heads jutting forward between the linked arms of the players in the row in front of them. The two "packs" thus formed faced off, and the players in the front row of each pack gripped the shirts of the opposing team's front-line players. The ball was rolled into a narrow tunnel on the ground between the intertwined packs. Players in the front rows attempted to kick the ball to their teammates, while each pack pushed in an attempt to physically gain the upper hand.

Camp proposed replacing the barely controlled chaos of the scrum with the scrimmage, which, as he described it, "takes place when the holder of the ball puts it on the ground before him and puts it in play while on-side either by kicking the ball or snapping it back with his foot. The man who first receives the ball from the snap-back shall be called the quarter-back." Kicking the ball backward proved awkward, leading some "holders" of the ball—centers as they are known today—to kick it a short distance, then pick it up and toss it to the quarterback. The practice of the center using his hands to toss the ball between his legs to the quarterback entered the game in 1894.

Adopting the scrimmage quickly proved to have unintended adverse consequences. In rugby, possession of the ball changed frequently, during a scrum, or when a player was brought down and was required to relinquish the ball, or when a team kicked away the ball to get out of a bad field position. But with the introduction of the scrimmage, one team could hold onto a ball indefinitely. The worst-case scenario occurred in a nightmarishly boring contest in 1881 between

127

Princeton and Yale, both of which didn't want to risk their undefeated records. Princeton had possession of the ball for the entire first half without making any significant moves or scoring. Yale did exactly the same during its possession in the second half, in what came to be called the "block" game.

To prevent football from becoming little more than a glorified game of keep-away, Camp developed the requirement that a team had to move the ball a minimum distance in a certain number of plays in order to retain possession: the concept of downs and yards to go. The new rule, adopted on October 12, 1882, originally allowed a team three tries to move the ball ahead five yards. (The team got to keep the ball if it lost ten yards or more in three tries.) The rule was revised in 1912 to four downs and ten yards.

Camp dropped out of Yale Medical School after two years and soon was working at the New Haven Clock Company, but he continued to be deeply involved in football in general and Yale football in particular. In 1883 he made another significant improvement by standardizing the scoring system for the game.

Camp's first set of rules awarded a team five points for a field goal, four for a goal kicked after a touchdown, two for a touchdown, and one for a safety. (The safety was a new method of scoring that Camp invented.) Before the year was out, the point system was revised. Although a field goal still put five points on the scoreboard, a touchdown was now worth four points, a kicked goal after a touchdown two points, and a safety two points. The current values of six points for a touchdown, one for a kick after the touchdown, three for a field goal, and two for a safety were in place by 1912.

By the end of 1884 Camp, still just twenty-five years old, had essentially invented what would become America's most popular spectator sport. Even while he worked conscientiously at his "real job," ultimately rising to be president and chairman of the board of the New Haven Clock Company, he continued to be a major force in shaping and refining football. With his support, tackling below the waist was made legal in 1888, and the forward pass was sanctioned in 1906.

As early as 1892 Camp was hailed as "the Father of American Football." But he was just getting started. He ventured into promoting football, carving out yet a third career as a sports writer. Camp published more than twenty-five books about football and other athletic pursuits, the first issued in 1886, and 250 magazine stories. He knew what he was talking about. During the quarter century he served as unofficial football coach, Yale teams were the undisputed champions of the gridiron, with a record of 218 wins, 11 losses, and 8 ties.

From 1878 until his death in 1925, Camp was a member of the organization that established the rules for college football in the United States. He was also one of the founders in 1906 of the National Collegiate Athletic Association, better known today by its acronym NCAA.

Walter Camp's legacy lives on in every football game in every stadium on any autumn day. It can be felt in fans' tense anticipation as their team goes to the line of scrimmage for a third-down-and-long situation, in the groaning when the ball carrier is brought down in his own end zone and two points for a safety are added to the opposing team's score, and in the roar of a cheering crowd leaping to its feet when the quarterback takes the snap from the center, falls back, and drills a pass into the end zone for a touchdown.

1888

The Great Blizzard

Writing in the Monday, March 12, 1888, issue of the *New Haven Evening Register*, a reporter used the alliterative adjectives "bewildering, belligerent, blinding" to describe the late-season snowstorm that had been pounding Connecticut since Sunday evening. By the time the storm ended on March 14, 1888, the reporter could have added two more adjectives to his description: historic and deadly.

The Blizzard of '88, as it came to be called, was the worst snowstorm in Connecticut history. Also known as "the Great White Hurricane," it dropped as much as fifty inches of the white stuff, which winds as high as sixty miles an hour sculpted into drifts up to thirty-eight feet tall. It brought not just Connecticut but almost the entire Northeast to a complete standstill and left more than four hundred people dead.

With scientific weather forecasting still in its infancy, there was no way the Northeast could have had any idea that a gigantic nor'easter was building over the second weekend in March. In fact, the weather had been springlike on Sunday, March 11. It turned cold later in the day, and by the evening snow began to fall in Connecticut.

March snow is nothing new in New England; people can be forgiven if they expected that a few inches, maybe more, would fall and then the storm would move on. But like an obnoxious houseguest who refuses to leave, the nor'easter sat stubbornly right over New England. It snowed all day Monday, all day Tuesday, and into Wednesday.

By the time the storm ended on March 14, most of Connecticut was covered with at least twenty inches of snow. Fifty inches—more than four feet—fell at Middletown. That was the highest amount recorded anywhere in Connecticut, and it tied with Saratoga Springs, New York, for the heaviest snowfall anywhere in the storm's path.

All forms of land transportation quickly came to a halt. Horsecars and stagecoaches couldn't make it through roads clogged with snow.

Even the mighty iron horse on its rails proved no match for the phenomenal snowfall. Some trains barely made it out of the station. Others managed to travel some distance before the going became too difficult, stranding passengers for hours and, in one case, for more than a day, with nearly nothing to eat. Hundreds of passengers were marooned in stations in cities such as Hartford and Bridgeport. Many a train was derailed in the effort to break through the wall of white.

The disruption of transportation didn't merely inconvenience travelers. Deliveries of food and fuel were interrupted.

Throughout it all, the vast majority of residents had no way of finding out what was going on beyond their home or immediate neighborhood. Telephones were a newfangled luxury that only the privileged few had in their houses. The telegraph lines that carried most communications between cities fell under the weight of the snow. All people could do was wait for the storm to end while wondering and worrying about what was happening in the rest of the world.

Those who ventured out into the blizzard put their lives in grave peril. Of the four hundred deaths attributed to the storm throughout the Northeast, half occurred in New York City, but Connecticut experienced the blizzard's deadly might as well. Many men and women—perhaps intrepid, perhaps unable to afford losing a day's wages—who somehow managed to make their way to the factories and shops where they were employed found that they could not perform their jobs because snow had accumulated on roofs in dangerous amounts or because supplies of fuel to power the machinery or to heat the buildings couldn't be delivered. The fuel shortage was a critical consideration, given that the temperatures at times dipped into the single digits.

Returning home, whether shortly after arriving or after putting in a day's work, meant running an even more dangerous gauntlet of snow, wind, and cold. Thirty female factory workers in Derby who decided to head for home "fell exhausted in the snowdrifts, and, would have perished speedily but for the bravery of citizens who organized themselves into a volunteer patrol and all night long went wading and watching through the bitter cold of the street," reported the *New York Times*. "One of the girls was not found till late at night. There is little hope that she can recover from the injuries that the blizzard inflicted."

Two Bridgeport women who headed home from the factory in which they worked on Monday night weren't as fortunate. They were found on Wednesday, frozen to death in a snowdrift a short distance from their workplace. Elsewhere in the city a fierce wind toppled a railroad signal tower, killing the man inside.

The situation was equally desperate in the countryside. In the Naugatuck Valley "hardy men have died from the exposure," reported the *New York Times* on March 18. "Horses and cattle have perished. Dwellings and barns have broken down."

The grim news was at times lightened by accounts of near miracles and savvy survivorship. In Waterford two siblings, just four and nine years old, became disoriented while trying to walk through the storm to their aunt's house, where their mother was. They took shelter beside a stone wall. Even though they were quickly covered by the rapidly accumulating snow, they managed to survive until searchers found them. Luckily, their only injuries were frostbite on their hands and ears.

When Joseph Jennings of New Haven could no longer continue to fight his way home from work through the snow on Tuesday, he had the presence of mind to burrow out a cave in a snowdrift, where he found sanctuary until the storm stopped.

When the blizzard finally ended, Connecticut residents found themselves confronted with a massive cleanup job that would have challenged the strength of Hercules. Back then, streets could be cleared by plows drawn by horses or oxen; otherwise they would have to be dug out by men wielding shovels. Another option for making roads passable was to use rollers, also pulled by horses or oxen, to pack down the snow so that sleds and sleighs could glide with ease.

Some people found themselves trapped in their homes by drifts that blocked doors. Sidewalks had to be cleared by shoveling. Snow removed from streets and sidewalks and tossed atop tall drifts formed gigantic, craggy, icy white mounds that resembled something from the Arctic. In a number of Connecticut communities, snow piles were tall and firm enough to be cut through by tunnels with enough clearance for a person to stand upright. These tunnels generally were not very long, suggesting that they were created as novelties rather than necessities.

Train tracks had to be cleared by hand to allow engines to resume movement. Derailed engines had to be dug out by men with shovels. Rail traffic was snarled for weeks in the wake of the blizzard.

Living through a historic event can make for exciting stories and memories, but it isn't necessarily pleasant at the time it happens. That reality was expressed by a group of Hartford men who fashioned an effigy of John Whitaker Watson, author of a popular poem of the era titled "Beautiful Snow," which contained lines such as "The town is alive and the heart in a glow / To welcome the coming of the beautiful snow." The men strung up the poet's effigy in front of a hotel, where men who had survived the most ferocious blizzard in New England history could release some of their storm-related frustration by pelting it with snowballs.

1910–1919

Arsenic and Multiple Homicide

The classic black comedy *Arsenic and Old Lace* is the tale of two sweetly dotty elderly spinster sisters who bring "peace" to lonely old men who come looking to rent a room in their house by serving them homemade elderberry wine spiked with a deadly dose of arsenic. But there was nothing amusing or quaintly quirky about the real-life murderess who inspired *Arsenic and Old Lace* playwright Joseph Kesselring. Amy Archer-Gilligan of Windsor was convicted of administering lethal amounts of the tasteless, odorless poison to one resident of her Windsor boardinghouse, almost certainly killed three others with arsenic, and may have been responsible for the deaths of many more.

The woman accused of operating a "murder factory" was born Amy Duggan in Litchfield, Connecticut, in 1868.

She was the seventh of ten children—nine daughters and one son—of Irish immigrants.

Amy Duggan married James Archer, a telegrapher and factory worker, around 1896. Their only child, a daughter named Mary, was born the next year.

In 1901 the Archers became live-in caretakers for widower John D. Seymour of Newington. After Seymour's death in 1904, the Archers stayed on, taking in elderly individuals until September 1907, when the Seymour house was sold. James and Amy bought a house on Prospect Street in Windsor and opened it in September 1907 as the Archer Home for Elderly People.

James Archer died on February 11, 1910, at the age of fifty-two, leaving Amy to run the Home. On November 25, 1913, the Widow Archer married Michael Gilligan. He died less than three months after the wedding, on February 20, 1914. The cause, according to his death certificate, was "valvular heart disease" and "acute bilious attack."

Mrs. Archer-Gilligan, as she was known after her second marriage, continued to operate the Archer Home as before. But the sudden, unexpected death of Archer Home "inmate" (as boarders were called) Franklin Andrews, age sixty-one, on May 30, 1914, raised questions that would lead to her trial for murder.

Inmates at the Archer Home could pay a weekly fee, ranging widely from $5 to $25, or could make a one-time payment of $1,000, which guaranteed them lifetime residence and care. However, calculated at the rates paid by weekly boarders, a life contract would cover expenses for only nine months at $25 a week or four years at $5 a week. A long-lived life-contract resident would come to constitute a financial drain on the Archer Home.

Franklin Andrews had come to live at the Archer Home for the Elderly in September 1912, under a life-care arrangement. On May 29, 1914, he was to all appearances in good health, puttering around the yard of the Archer Home, as he often did. But at five o'clock on the morning of May 30, he woke up vomiting.

Mrs. Archer-Gilligan didn't call a doctor for Andrews until late in the afternoon. By the time she summoned the physician a second time, at 9:00 p.m., Andrews was dead.

Around 11:00 p.m. Mrs. Archer-Gilligan called Franklin Andrews's sister, Mrs. Nellie Pierce, to tell her he was sick but assured her that his condition wasn't grave enough to warrant her coming immediately to Windsor from her home in Hartford. In fact, Mrs. Archer-Gilligan had already arranged for his body to be transported immediately to a Hartford funeral home without securing the required legal permit.

Mrs. Pierce arrived in Windsor early the next morning and was told that her brother had died shortly after Mrs. Archer-Gilligan's telephone call the previous evening. Despite Mrs. Archer-Gilligan's insensitive and inappropriate conduct regarding the death of Franklin Andrews, foul play was not immediately suspected. Then in June Mrs. Pierce found in her brother's effects a letter from Mrs. Archer-Gilligan, written about a month before his death. In it Mrs. Archer-Gilligan asked Andrews for a loan of "as near $1,000 as possible" by the next day to pay bills left by her late husband. She also requested that Andrews "say nothing to any one about the matter."

When Mrs. Pierce discovered that her brother had withdrawn $500 from the bank at the time of the request, she confronted Mrs. Archer-Gilligan, who first said that the loan had never been made but then changed her story to say Andrews had given her $500 "as a gift to the home." After Mrs. Pierce retained a lawyer, Mrs. Archer-Gilligan repaid the $500, claiming she did it only to avoid a fight and not because she felt obliged to do so.

Mrs. Pierce took her now thoroughly aroused suspicions about her brother's death to State's Attorney Hugh Alcorn in the summer of 1914. When Alcorn told her he didn't see sufficient evidence to justify an investigation by his office, Mrs. Pierce turned to the *Hartford Courant* newspaper.

After looking into the death of Franklin Andrews for several months, the *Courant* turned its findings over to the state police. In the spring of 1915, Captain Robert Hurley began what would be a nearly yearlong investigation that took him to more than twenty towns and out of state. Captain Hurley strove to keep a low profile to avoid tipping off Mrs. Archer-Gilligan to the fact that she was being investigated.

Finally, on May 2, 1916, the body of Franklin Andrews was exhumed from his grave in a Cheshire burial ground under cover of darkness, and a "secret" autopsy was conducted in the cemetery tool house by the light of two lanterns. "The lack of decomposition of the body was remarkable considering it had been buried about two years," according to the *Courant*. The condition of the corpse was a possible sign of poisoning by arsenic, which could preserve a dead body.

Andrews's stomach and other organs were put in jars and taken to Hartford for analysis. Although Andrews's death certificate said he had died from gastric ulcers, none were found. Tests revealed that Andrews's organs contained enough arsenic to kill at least three men and that it had been administered in two doses, one about ten hours before his death, the second shortly before he expired.

Captain Hurley arrested Mrs. Archer-Gilligan for the first-degree murder of Franklin Andrews on May 8, 1916. "She took the news calmly," reported the *Courant*, "and claimed, 'I will prove my innocence.'"

The photograph of Mrs. Archer-Gilligan that illustrated the *Courant*'s front-page article breaking the story showed a square-jawed woman with deep-set eyes and a high forehead framed by an abundance of dark hair. She wore a solemn, almost stern expression. The accused was reportedly a small woman, a few inches over five feet and weighing no more than 115 pounds. Although the *Courant* said she was forty-one, she had conveniently shaved seven years off her age and was in fact forty-eight.

The circumstances of Franklin Andrews's demise, and the fact that more than four dozen residents of the Archer Home had died in the six years prior to Mrs. Archer-Gilligan's arrest, prompted authorities to look more closely at the deaths of several other people—including Mrs. Archer-Gilligan's second husband.

Michael Gilligan had been in good health until just a few days before his death. The day before he died, he had signed a will, drafted by his wife, leaving everything he owned to her. Although the will had been declared invalid because it was not witnessed by the required three people, Mrs. Archer-Gilligan was named executor of the estate. After some squabbling, an agreement was reached in which Michael Gilligan's relatives received a portion of his estate and the rest went to Mrs. Archer-Gilligan.

Michael Gilligan's body was exhumed on July 1, 1916, from St. Mary's Cemetery in Windsor Locks. Analysis revealed the cause of death to be arsenic poisoning. Three more bodies—those of Charles A. Smith, who died April 9,

1914; Mrs. Alice Gowdy, who died December 14, 1914; and Mrs. Maud Howard Lynch, who died February 2, 1916— were exhumed in order to test for poison. Both Mr. Smith and Mrs. Gowdy had arsenic in their stomachs, while Mrs. Lynch's death had been caused by strychnine.

Mrs. Archer-Gilligan was indicted for all five murders. In June 1917 she was put on trial only for the death of Franklin Andrews, to which she pleaded not guilty.

Evidence introduced by the prosecution to connect Mrs. Archer-Gilligan to the poisonings included records from a Windsor drugstore showing that over a one-year period the accused woman had purchased more than one and a half pounds of arsenic, allegedly for killing rats. She had bought some arsenic three days before her second husband's death and had purchased two ounces of arsenic four days before Franklin Andrews died.

Even more damning was the testimony of Loren Gowdy, widower of Alice Gowdy. He stated that in May 1914 he and his wife had visited the Archer Home to explore the possibility of taking up residence there. They told Mrs. Archer-Gilligan they would come only if they could have the room then occupied by Franklin Andrews and his roommate. Mrs. Archer-Gilligan told them they could have the room by June 1.

After Franklin Andrews's conveniently timed death on May 30, Mrs. Archer-Gilligan sent the Gowdys a telegram informing them that the room they wanted was now available. The couple moved in, but Mrs. Gowdy apparently became one of the homicidal landlady's victims, dying on December 14, 1914, of arsenic poisoning.

It took a jury just four hours of deliberation to find Amy Archer-Gilligan guilty of first-degree murder on July 13, 1917. She was sentenced to be hanged on November 6.

The governor of Connecticut granted a reprieve of the death sentence while Mrs. Archer-Gilligan's attorney appealed the verdict. On April 30, 1918, a new trial was granted, based on the fact that in the original proceeding the prosecution had introduced evidence about the poisoning deaths of individuals other than Franklin Andrews, for whose murder alone Mrs. Archer-Gilligan was on trial.

In her new trial Mrs. Archer-Gilligan's counsel put forth insanity as the defense. A doctor who had known the Duggan family in Litchfield for decades testified that three of Mrs. Archer-Gilligan's siblings were insane, including a brother with "tendencies" toward homicide who had been committed to the Connecticut Hospital for the Insane in Middletown. Three "alienists," as experts on mental illness were then known, testified that Mrs. Archer-Gilligan was insane, and that her mental instability was aggravated by an addiction to morphine, which had been purchased at the same drugstore where she bought arsenic.

The proceedings reached a sudden, unexpected, and dramatic climax on July 1, 1919. In a hastily arranged deal, Mrs. Archer-Gilligan pleaded guilty to second-degree murder. She was sentenced to life in the Wethersfield Prison.

Years later, Mrs. Archer-Gilligan was transferred from prison to the Connecticut Hospital for the Insane in Middletown. There she died in 1962, at the age of ninety-four.

Playwright Joseph Kesselring learned of Archer-Gilligan's sensational story and trials through coverage that appeared in newspapers across the nation. On a visit to Hartford, Kesselring was able to examine the court records. This bizarre tale of one woman's secret series of multiple homicides by poisoning provided Kesselring with grist for *Arsenic and Old Lace*, which opened on Broadway in January

1941. Legendary director Frank Capra directed the 1944 film version, starring Cary Grant, Peter Lorre, and Raymond Massey. The setting was Brooklyn, New York, not Connecticut, and the poisonous protagonists were motivated only by misguided compassion, not the avarice that drove Amy Archer-Gilligan.

1975

A Lady Governor, but Never a Governor's First Lady

Today, when a woman is elected governor of a state, her gender is a minor part—if that—of the story. After all, a woman is vice president of the United States, a woman was the Democratic nominee for president in 2016, and dozens of women have occupied the chief executive's chair of states from Alaska to Alabama, from Utah to Vermont. Not so very long ago, however, it was a much different situation. In 1974, when Connecticut citizens voted Ella Grasso into office as governor, it was major news that made headlines across the nation.

Ella Grasso, however, was not the first woman to be governor of a state. That distinction belongs to Nellie Tayloe Ross, who was elected governor of Wyoming in 1924 in a special election called to fill the vacancy left by the death of her husband, Governor William Ross.

Two weeks after Nellie Tayloe Ross took office in Wyoming in 1925, the United States got its second female governor. Miriam Amanda Ferguson was elected governor of Texas in a campaign during which she made clear her intention to be guided while in office by her husband, James Ferguson. He had been governor of Texas from 1915 to 1917, until he was impeached, convicted, removed from office, and barred from ever holding a state position.

The third woman to be elected governor of a state was Lurleen Wallace of Alabama. Alabama law forbade her husband, Governor George Wallace, from running for a second consecutive term in 1966. Lurleen Wallace ran in George's place, was elected, and served until 1968, when she died in office from cancer.

Ella Grasso, by contrast, was, in her own succinct phrase, "the first lady governor who was not a governor's first lady." Her husband was an educator who never held elective office. When people voted for Grasso for governor, they were voting for her, for the fifty-six-year-old career public servant, not some spouse who would call the shots from behind the scenes.

Ella Grasso's rise to the state's highest elective office was all the more remarkable because of her background. Ella Giovanna Oliva Tambussi's parents were Italian immigrants who had entered the United States through Ellis Island less than twenty years before their only child was born in Windsor Locks, Connecticut, in 1919. Her father worked in factories and later owned and operated a bakery.

Grasso's parents' commitment to education and her own hard work earned her access to the finest private schools, including the Chaffee School in Windsor and Mount Holyoke College, where she earned a bachelor's degree (graduating magna cum laude and having been elected to Phi Beta Kappa) and a master of arts degree. The year she received her graduate degree, 1942, she married Tom Grasso, a teacher. The couple would have a son and a daughter.

From her first job out of college with the state's War Manpower Commission to her election as governor, Ella Grasso spent her entire professional life working either in government or for the Democratic Party—although she initially was a registered Republican and remained one until the 1950 election. She climbed the rungs of the political ladder slowly but steadily: election to the Connecticut State House of Representatives in 1952, to the office of Secretary of the State in 1959, to the U.S. House of Representatives in 1970 and again in 1972.

But Grasso was unhappy in the relatively powerless position of a congresswoman with little seniority. In 1974 she decided to seek the Connecticut governorship. After defeating a rival for the Democratic Party's nomination, Grasso was elected the eighty-third governor of Connecticut by a decisive margin of 200,000 votes. She had, as a Connecticut magazine writer noted, "conquered the oldest bastion of male chauvinism in Connecticut: the governor's office."

Grasso's shattering of a significant political "glass ceiling" was hailed as a profound step forward for women. It was covered internationally by major media, from *Time* magazine to *Ladies' Home Journal* to *People* magazine, but it meant relatively little to Grasso personally. "The fact of my gender has not been a pressing issue in my life," she observed the year after she became governor of Connecticut. At another time she commented, "I don't give any quarter, and I don't expect any as a woman. I expect to be treated as a person and I usually am."

Upon taking office in 1975, Grasso found herself head of a state that was $70 million in debt. The steps she took to try to rein in the budget earned her the enmity of a variety of groups, although she was eventually successful in balancing the books.

In 1976, the year of the nation's bicentennial, there was talk of Grasso as a possible Democratic candidate for vice president—even president. But Grasso had her sights set on a second term as governor—which was far from a sure thing.

And then came the Blizzard of 1978. One of the worst winter storms in Connecticut history, the eighteen inches of snow it delivered were whipped into towering drifts by fifty-mile-per-hour winds.

Ella Grasso immediately took command of the situation. She declared state roads closed for three days to allow crews to clear them, an action that had the ripple effect of shutting down just about everything else in Connecticut. She oversaw distribution of supplies, sought help from the federal government, and kept the press—and through them the people—apprised of the situation as it unfolded.

Grasso surveyed the devastation firsthand from National Guard helicopters. The impression citizens received of her during this natural disaster—of a governor who cared, who took action, who was there when people needed her—was captured in a photograph of the words "Ella Help!" stamped into the snow in a Norwich field as an appeal that could be read from the air.

Her virtuoso performance in the blizzard crisis went a long way toward increasing Grasso's positive image among voters. She won reelection as governor easily in 1978, by more than 189,000 votes.

She entered into a second term fraught with as many problems, if not more, than her first one, although she now had a budget surplus. She addressed poverty, mass transit, child care, and the needs of the state's elderly. She dealt with the crippling impact on Connecticut of a gasoline shortage that required rationing, and again she was called upon to respond to a natural disaster when a tornado ripped through her hometown of Windsor Locks and neighboring communities. Despite her best efforts, skyrocketing energy costs and unemployment resulting from a sluggish economy put Connecticut $128 million in the red, forcing her to propose an increase in the state sales tax.

Then in March 1980, a little more than a year into her second term as governor, Grasso was diagnosed with ovarian cancer. By the end of the year, it had spread to her liver. She resigned as governor effective December 31, 1980, and died six weeks later.

Thousands of Connecticut citizens stood in long lines for hours in a cold February rain to view Ella Grasso's coffin as it lay in state in the State Capitol. President Jimmy Carter sent words of praise: "Her career stands as a testament to the good that government can do and to the difference one person can make."

Born before American females were even permitted to vote, Ella Grasso had, whether she intended to or not, blazed a trail for women in politics. It had taken 198 years from the colonies' Declaration of Independence for a woman to be elected governor of a state "in her own right," as it is often phrased. Just two years would pass following Grasso's victory before another woman would be elected governor in her own right: Dixy Lee Ray, who was voted into the chief executive office of the State of Washington in 1976. As of 2022, more than 40 women had been elected governor of one of the United States.

In 1987, a life-size marble statue of Ella Grasso was installed in one of 26 niches included for such a purpose on the exterior of the Connecticut State Capitol in Hartford. She was the first woman to be so honored, joining sculptures of such Connecticut luminaries as signers of the Declaration of Independence Roger Sherman and Oliver Wolcott, Sr., and pioneering lexicographer Noah Webster. As of 2022, Grasso remains the only woman to occupy one of those niches.

1978

Miraculous Disaster

It was one of the greatest disasters ever to happen in Hartford. But thanks to divine intervention, or fate, or luck, or chance, or whatever, the collapse of the roof of the Hartford Civic Center Coliseum on January 18, 1978, narrowly missed being a tragedy—possibly the most massive tragedy in Connecticut history.

The Coliseum, with seating for 12,500 spectators, was the anchor of the grandly named Hartford Civic Center Veterans Memorial Coliseum and Exhibition Center, a $70 million project that in turn had been built as the centerpiece of the city's latest downtown renewal effort. Since the Coliseum's opening in 1975, it had presented concerts by the biggest stars in show business and hosted an array of conventions. It was home ice to the New England Whalers of the professional World Hockey

Association. The Boston Celtics professional basketball team played part of their regular season schedule at the Coliseum, as did the University of Connecticut men's basketball team.

On the night of Tuesday, January 17, 1978, five thousand spectators had watched the University of Connecticut men's basketball team defeat the University of Massachusetts team. By midnight the fans were all gone, and the Coliseum was deserted, a rare situation.

Often after a basketball game, workers had to labor overnight to convert the court into a hockey rink for a Whalers game the next day. But it so happened that the Celtics had played the Coliseum the previous night, and a high school basketball game was scheduled for Wednesday, so the changeover from hardwood to ice had not been required.

At 4:15 a.m. on Wednesday, January 18, the few people who were up and about in the predawn darkness in the vicinity of the Civic Center were startled by a sudden, sharp cracking sound followed by a thunderous crash. The center of the Coliseum's roof had given way and plummeted eighty-three feet straight down to the ground.

As the center fell, the roof's four corners were forced upward. To someone looking down on the site from the upper stories of any of the nearby high-rises, it roughly resembled a massive metal soufflé that had fallen in the middle. A local businessman said that it looked as if a meteorite had slammed into the Coliseum.

The carnage that would have resulted if the 1,400-ton steel roof had given way just eight hours earlier or eight hours later was almost too terrible to contemplate. The Civic Center's then assistant general manager, Frank Russo, has been quoted as recalling, "Some of the beams came down like arrows. They would hit a seat and go through three feet of concrete then thirty feet down into the floor of the exhibition hall to create an eight-or nine-inch dent in a solid ground level concrete floor." As it was, not a single person was killed or even injured in the collapse.

After relief that no lives had been lost passed, the immediate question was, why had it happened? Why had the Coliseum roof, completed in 1973, just five years earlier, failed so suddenly and completely?

The 108,000-square-foot roof had been a space frame—a design that allows for fewer supporting columns that would interfere with the audience's view of the court or stage. A subsequent investigation revealed that, in the case of the Civic Center Coliseum, alterations and errors both large and small in the design, prepared with state-of-the art computer software, and in construction, the result primarily of time- and cost-saving measures, contributed to the collapse. Underestimating the weight of the roof itself by one-fifth when calculating the load that would have to be supported was just one of those mistakes.

There were indications that something was amiss during construction. While the roof was being pieced together on the ground, an inspector informed the building's designers that a troubling deviation from the specifications had been observed. No action was taken. When the roof was raised and put into place, that deviation was again noted.

Again, the designers were not worried. A subcontractor who had trouble completing his part of the roof project because of the deviation was instructed by the project manager to simply deal with the problem or else take the blame for holding up the job.

The result was that the Coliseum's flawed roof began to fail from the day it was finished. It was a disaster waiting to happen.

Winter supplied the proverbial straw that broke the camel's back. Ten inches of snow had fallen in Hartford on January 17—the biggest single snowfall since the Coliseum's roof had been built. Added to what had accumulated from previous snowfalls, the load on the roof was at most seventy-three pounds per square foot. If constructed properly, the roof should have been able to withstand nearly twice that weight. However, the design and construction errors and changes had severely compromised the roof's weightbearing capacity.

Even without any casualties, the Coliseum roof collapse was a devastating blow to Greater Hartford. More than three hundred concerts, sporting events, and conventions planned for the Coliseum would now take place somewhere else besides Hartford, thus depriving city hotels, restaurants, and merchants of much-needed collateral income.

Plans to replace the Coliseum were under way within twenty-four hours of the roof's collapse. Hartford City Manager James Daken sketched out a concept on an envelope. He then called a press conference to inform the media that a "bigger and better" Coliseum would be constructed, adding that "it will have a different kind of roof." Two years later Daken's commitment was fulfilled. (Since 2007 the Hartford Civic Center, of which the rebuilt Veterans Memorial Coliseum is a part, has been officially called the XL Center.)

Four more years would pass before the City of Hartford accepted a $1.8 million settlement from a lawsuit filed against the contractor, the engineers, and the architects. More than four decades after it happened, the 1978 Civic Center Coliseum roof collapse is remembered as an incredible, breathtaking event—but thanks to a miracle of timing, not a heartbreaking one.

1991

Hangin' with the Governor

On an autumn Saturday in October 1991, in front of the gold-domed State Capitol in Hartford, before one of the largest crowds ever in Connecticut history, a centuries-old custom was revived: hanging a public official in effigy. The issue that inspired protesters to hoist a straw dummy of Connecticut Governor Lowell P. Weicker Jr. on a gibbet that day was the same one that had motivated colonists to string up effigies of a royal appointee more than 220 years earlier: taxes.

In the spring of 1765 word reached Connecticut that the British Parliament had voted to levy a tax on a wide range of paper items such as newspapers, legal documents, and even playing cards that were used in Britain's North American colonies. A stamp attached to the item would prove that the tax had been paid; hence the legislation was called the Stamp

Act. Great Britain, hugely in debt following its victory in the Seven Years' War, looked to the Stamp Act to raise revenue to fund British troops assigned to guard its North American colonies' western wilderness borders.

Colonists were enraged at the tax, which had been imposed on them by a legislature to which they were not allowed to send any delegates and thus in whose decisions they had no voice. They made certain that their objections to the Stamp Act would nonetheless be heard loud and clear in London by staging massive protest meetings around the colony.

On August 22, 1765, an effigy of the man who had agreed to act as distributor of the stamps in Connecticut "was exhibited on a Gallows erected for that Purpose, in the most publick Part" of New London. It was then paraded on a pole down Main Street, "accompanied with various Kinds of Musick, Guns, Drums, &c. and incessant Acclamations of the Multitude . . . an evident Demonstration of their Thirst for LIBERTY, and Detestation of STAMP-ACTS," reported the *Connecticut Courant*. In Windham on August 26, the stamp distributor also "made his Appearance in Effigie, suspended between the Heavens and the Earth," according to the *Courant*, which also reported that in Lebanon, on August 27, an effigy was given a mock trial and then was dragged to "the place of Execution [and] hanged by the Neck 'til dead."

These and other, sometimes more violent, protests in Connecticut and throughout all the other colonies had their desired effect. In 1766 Parliament repealed the Stamp Act. It proved to be a meaningless victory, however. The British government persisted in imposing new taxes on the colonies, both to bring in money and to press home the point that its wishes trumped those of its subjects in North

America. It was a contest of wills and principles that led to the American Revolution and an independent United States of America.

Fast-forward 226 years. The State of Connecticut was facing a budget deficit estimated at the time of the 1990 election to be the staggering figure of $250 million. Lowell P. Weicker Jr., who had represented Connecticut in the U.S. Senate as a Republican for eighteen years, was elected governor that November, running as the candidate of his own independent third party. Weicker had stated during the campaign that he was "opposed" to addressing the fiscal crisis by introducing a state income tax—a topic that could be described as the "third rail" of Connecticut politics.

By the time Weicker was sworn in as governor on January 9, 1991, estimates of the deficit had ballooned to close to $1 billion, and projections for future shortfalls were, if possible, even grimmer. The newly inaugurated governor concluded that the solution to what he considered the "worst fiscal crisis in Connecticut since the Great Depression" had to include a state income tax.

Following six months of difficult, sometimes rancorous, negotiation, both houses of the General Assembly passed, by narrow margins, a six percent state income tax, to take effect October 1, 1991. The governor signed it.

Opponents called for a massive rally to demand repeal of the unpopular tax. The stage was set for the comeback of the effigy.

On the morning of October 6, 1991, the crowd began to amass around the State Capitol. "As in an old western, a scaffold showed up out of nowhere and a dummy looking like me was hung from it," Weicker wrote in his 1995 autobiography, *Maverick: A Life in Politics*.

Whoever crafted the straw effigy had gone to some trouble to make it a reasonable facsimile of the governor, dressing it in slacks, a long-sleeve dress shirt, and a tie. Attached to its chest was a sign that read: POLITICAL DEATH TO TAX HIKER WEICKER!

Other signs throughout the growing crowd demanded that the governor be impeached or called for "A GOVERNOR NOT A KING." One proposing to "CUT GOV. FAT. START WITH LOWELL WEICKER" was a reference to the six-foot, six-inch-tall governor's hefty build.

Late in the morning, with the crowd still far from its peak size, Governor Lowell Weicker in the flesh approached the State Capitol from the nearby Legislative Office Building. Accompanied by his chief of staff and a plainclothes state policeman, the sixty-year-old governor waded into the crowd. He engaged a dozen or more individuals in discussions that he characterized as "honest disagreements, honest questions."

But as Weicker rounded the front of the Capitol into the expanding crowd, the situation became increasingly tense, then ugly. Some protesters spat on Weicker; some swore at him. "Now mob psychology took hold. . . . Many of these plain folks took on a violent, threatening air," recalled Weicker. Some became physically aggressive.

Several more plainclothes troopers moved in to protect Weicker. Finally, at a sign from his chief of staff, the officers steered Weicker through the press of people and into the State Capitol. Weicker was not happy at being hustled away from the crowd. "More important than personal safety at that moment was the symbolic presence of the governor at this 'petitioning' of the government," he said.

That "petitioning" of the government, estimated to have grown by mid-afternoon to at least forty thousand people, and perhaps as many as sixty-five thousand, covered the entire front lawn of the State Capitol and spilled out onto the street. "With Connecticut's population of about 3.3 million, more than one out of every 100 residents had come to shout and cheer, to rage about the tax and exult at what speaker after speaker said was the power to repeal the law, just waiting to be grasped," reported Kirk Johnson in the *New York Times*.

Despite the enormous numbers and the fever-pitch emotions, the protest came off without major incident. The citizens of Connecticut had exercised their First Amendment right "peaceably to assemble, and to petition the Government for a redress of grievances."

Unlike their counterparts in 1765, the tax protesters of 1991 did not achieve their goal. Efforts to repeal the state income tax failed, and more than thirty years later it remains in effect.

There was another fundamental difference between the tax protests of the eighteenth century and that of the late twentieth. The colonists were expressing their opposition to "taxation without representation." The 1991 tax protesters were enraged about an income tax that, however unfair and burdensome it was in their eyes, had been passed into law by the representatives and senators elected by the people of Connecticut to represent them in the General Assembly.

And about those effigies. The ones strung up and paraded around in 1765 in New London, Windham, and Lebanon all ended up being consumed by bonfires that were part of the protest. Lowell Weicker's was spared that fate. The day after the massive 1991 rally, quick-thinking staff members of the Raymond Baldwin Museum of Connecticut History, located in the Connecticut State Library building just across the street from the State Capitol, rescued the discarded effigy and added it to the collection of artifacts. Thanks to their intervention, tax protesters in the year 2217 will have something on which to model their own revival of an old colonial custom.

2002-TODAY

Remembering 9/11

On a morning as sunny and sparkling as September 11, 2001, staff and visitors at Sherwood Island State Park in Westport on Long Island Sound had a particularly clear view of the majestic Manhattan skyline forty-five miles to the southwest. For the past three decades, that splendid vista had been dominated by the two skyscrapers of the World Trade Center, at more than 1,360 feet high the tallest buildings in New York City.

But those who came to the park that shining Tuesday were stunned to see smoke filling a gap in the panorama where the twin towers had stood for so long. The smoke was rising, as it would continue to do for days afterward, from the rubble left after terrorists hijacked two passenger jets and deliberately flew them into the World Trade Center, bringing the complete collapse of both 110-story towers in less than two hours.

Even before the true enormity of the catastrophe could be fully comprehended, Connecticut officials immediately mobilized the state's resources to help the stricken Big Apple in any way. Connecticut Governor John Rowland and the state's Office of Emergency Management designated Sherwood Island State Park as the gathering point for heavy construction equipment, trucks, helicopters, and other vehicles to wait to be dispatched to help clear the rubble and search for survivors. National Guardsmen, paramedics, and firefighters prepared to respond the moment they were called to wherever in Manhattan they were needed. Hospitals across Connecticut rearranged patients and schedules to make available nine hundred beds to receive any of the injured that New York City's medical facilities couldn't accommodate.

But as the hours passed, and then a day, those hospital beds remained empty. Emergency medical and rescue personnel and equipment operators waited in vain for the summons that never came. In different circumstances such an absence of activity might have been seen as evidence that the tragedy's toll wouldn't be as great as had been originally feared. In this case, though, a much grimmer truth was becoming clear. Of the people who hadn't been able to escape the twin towers before they collapsed—including a total of four hundred emergency personnel, firefighters, and police officers —all but a very few had been killed in the fall. The fatalities included dozens of men and women from Connecticut.

Terrorists had also hijacked two other passenger airliners on the morning of September 11. One had struck the Pentagon outside Washington, D.C.; the other had crashed in a remote field in southwestern Pennsylvania, forced down by an uprising of the passengers before the terrorists could slam it into another target—possibly the U.S. Capitol. After weeks of agonizing searching of the rubble at all three crash sites, forensic testing, and frantic efforts to locate friends and family who were known or suspected to have been at the World Trade Center, at the Pentagon, or on board the hijacked planes that fateful morning, the total number of dead from the attacks of 9/11 stood at 2,974.

Of the dead, it was ultimately determined that 161 either lived in or had close ties to Connecticut. Many were from southwestern Connecticut, from which thousands of people commute to work in Manhattan every day.

As the initial shock of the tragedy subsided, thoughts began to turn to establishing an official memorial in Connecticut, which had been hit so hard in many ways by the horrific events so close to home. The Office of Family Support, created by the Connecticut Office of Policy and Management to provide assistance to relatives of 9/11 victims, spearheaded the effort.

The U.S. Congress, foreseeing a groundswell of interest in commemorating the deadliest enemy attack ever on American soil, had asked the U.S. Forest Service to create a "Living Memorials Project." Such an endeavor "invokes the resonating power of trees to bring people together and create lasting, living memorials to the victims of terrorism, their families, communities, and the nation," explains the project's website.

Members of Connecticut families affected by 9/11 expressed a desire for the memorial to be near the water and to face toward New York City. In the spring of 2002, the Connecticut Department of Environmental Protection gave permission for Sherwood Island State Park, with its special association with the World Trade Center in both good times and bad, to serve as the location for the Living Memorial.

Less than a year after the horrific attacks, funding from the U.S. Forest Service, along with private donations of time and materials, had created a commemorative site that evokes both the tragedy of the lives lost and the will of those left behind to continue on, always carrying with them the memories of those who died.

The memorial, which encompasses about one-third of an acre, consists of a nine-foot-long piece of granite, set in a grassy, landscaped area on the park's "point"—a small slice of land that juts out about three hundred feet into Long Island Sound. It was dedicated on September 5, 2002. The inscription reads: "THE CITIZENS OF CONNECTI-CUT DEDICATE THIS LIVING MEMORIAL TO THE THOUSANDS OF INNOCENT LIVES LOST ON SEP-TEMBER 11, 2001, AND TO THE FAMILIES WHO LOVED THEM." Visitors to what is Connecticut's official 9/11 memorial site need only lift their eyes to see in the distance the Manhattan cityscape that was so radically altered by the events of that day. "The view, not the stone, is the real 'monument,'" according to landscape architect Ron Clapper of the Connecticut Department of Environmental Protection State Parks Division, who was a member of the team that designed the memorial.

The design also included four granite benches as well as pine and hackberry trees. The memorial "incorporates the endurance of granite, the sheltering beauty of trees and shrubs, and the tranquility of the sea," explains the Department of Environmental Protection's website on the 9/11 Living Memorial.

Before a second year passed, the name of each of the Connecticut victims was carved on its own separate flat granite square and set into the ground, in rows that flank the main memorial stone. This new feature was dedicated during ceremonies in September 2003. As happens at the Vietnam Veterans' Memorial in Washington, visitors sometimes leave little mementoes, such as stones, shells, and flowers, on the plaque commemorating a loved one for whom there is no grave.

Connecticut has kept the memory of the lives lost that day fresh. On September 11, 2011, a sculpture titled "Sanctuary" was installed in a pavilion at the Sherwood Island site. It is composed of 10 blossoms, one for each year since the terrorist attack, with petals fashioned from pieces of metal recovered from the World Trade Center. It surrounds "bioplaques," with brief information such as age at the time of death for each of the victims, installed at the same time.

1800s–TODAY

The Nutmeg State

Connecticut sports the nickname of the "Nutmeg State," with its residents consequently being known as "Nutmeggers." This sobriquet has been incorporated into the names of everything from financial institutions to car dealerships to exterminators. One advertising campaign even morphed it into a verb: "nutmegging."

Why is a New England state nicknamed after the seed of a plant that grows only in places thousands of miles away, such as the Caribbean and the East Indies? The "Nutmeg State" moniker is rooted in the activities two centuries ago of an army of adventurous entrepreneurs whose ranks allegedly included some con men.

The small, hard, oval-shaped, brown, slightly wrinkled nutmeg is native to the East Indies. When grated, it produces a powder that is used as a spice in a variety of recipes and that was also believed to have medicinal properties. For centuries the East Indies were the only source of nutmeg, making it rare and expensive.

Nutmeg trees were introduced to the Caribbean island of Grenada in the early 1780s (today a nutmeg adorns Grenada's official flag). Connecticut merchants, who had been trading with the West Indies for decades, began to include them in the cargoes they brought on ships returning home to ports such as Middletown, Hartford, and New London.

Roughly around the same time, young men from New England began hitting the road as peddlers. One of the early catalysts for this development was the establishment of the American tin industry in Berlin, Connecticut, in the 1740s. Once the local demand for tin plates, spoons, and pots had been satiated, the next logical step was to open up new markets farther away.

Tin peddlers by the hundreds fanned out from Connecticut into other states, going door-to-door with their goods and their smooth sales pitch. To their stock they added all manner of hard-to-get items that would tempt residents of small towns and isolated farms: "Yankee notions" such as needles, pins, ribbons, buttons, and beads; cigars; clocks (once Connecticut inventors figured out how to make them small enough to carry)—and nutmegs. Peddlers often carried tin graters to use on the nutmegs.

By 1820 peddlers were a familiar sight on back roads throughout the eastern half of North America, from Canada to Kentucky to Missouri to Louisiana. Not all New England peddlers were from Connecticut, but the fact that so many were, combined with peddling's early association with the Connecticut-based tin industry, resulted in "peddler" or "Yankee peddler" becoming nearly synonymous with Connecticut.

A hardworking, ambitious peddler could make a tidy sum on a sales trip—especially if he knew how to drive a hard bargain. Peddling was typically a young man's job, something to be pursued for a few years before moving on to a less demanding, more stable occupation, possibly bankrolled by what he had earned during his years on the road.

Tales began to circulate about avaricious peddlers who took advantage of or cheated customers outright to maximize their profit. There were stories of peddlers who sold unsophisticated rural folk tin as silver, cigars made of oak leaves, clocks that quit running within days of their purchase, and an assortment of fake items fashioned of wood, including cheeses, hams, candles—and, for some reason the most common, nutmegs.

Reports of Yankee peddlers vending wooden nutmegs appeared in newspapers as early as 1817. According to one news item, in Columbus, Ohio, "A short time since, there passed through this place a pedlar, having among other articles, wooden Nutmegs for sale! It is reported that there actually were some of them purchased in this place. We have often heard of Yankee speculation, but conceive this to be about the climax." The next year, according to a Baltimore newspaper, Pennsylvania levied a tax on every tin peddler, commenting that "the good citizens of that state have not forgotten the wooden nutmeg cheat played off upon them last year, and are determined to guard against it hereafter."

An article in the *Baltimore Patriot* newspaper in 1823 on "Sectional Prejudices & Epithets" observed, "The south derives its notions of the manners of the north, and vice versa, too much from traders, pedlars, &c. so confine their observations to the circle of their avocations and are incompetent tourists. A Virginian buys a wooden nutmeg of 'a Yankee Pedlar,' and proscribes in 'one fell swoop' the whole people of New England—it was a 'Yankee trick—they are ALL SHARPERS.'" Six years later, the *National Intelligencer* newspaper explained that the phrase "damn Yankee" had gained currency among "the mass of the people, who derive their notions of 'the Yankees' from tin-pedlars and wooden-nutmeg venders."

The wooden nutmeg charge got even wider circulation when it appeared in works of popular fiction. In one 1832 novel, a Yankee peddler was put on trial for "selling, in the course of one peddling expedition, 497,368 wooden nutmegs."

As animosity between North and South grew in the decades preceding the Civil War, the wooden nutmeg charge may have taken on a sharper edge, having been transformed from a quaint characteristic to a contemptuous slur. South Carolina native Daniel Harvey Hill, a distinguished professor at Davidson College in North Carolina, who later became a general in the Confederate army, included in an algebra textbook he wrote in 1857 the following problem: "A Yankee mixes a certain number of wooden nutmegs, which cost him ¼ cent apiece, with a quantity of real nutmegs, worth 4 cents apiece, and sells the whole assortment for $44; and gains $3.75 by the fraud. How many wooden nutmegs were there?"

By now the Nutmeg State nickname had been permanently affixed to Connecticut. In 1859 *Bartlett's Dictionary of Americanisms* reported that it was "in allusion to the story that wooden nutmegs are there manufactured for exportation."

It may have been around this time of growing sectional strife that Connecticut residents began to embrace "wooden nutmeg state" or simply "nutmeg state." Just as rebels during the American Revolution had taken the sting out of the British song "Yankee Doodle," which mocked them as unsophisticated bumpkins, by adopting it as their own, so Connecticut citizens may have assumed as a badge of distinction the derogatory term applied to them for decades by the southerners who sought to split the Union.

When the *Hartford Daily Courant* reported on April 30, 1861, just fifteen days after the start of the Civil War, that the state had already raised four regiments of volunteers for the Union army, it commented: "We consider that we live in about as patriotic and loyal a Commonwealth as they have in this country. Three cheers for the little nutmeg State!" A Connecticut soldier in the Union army in Baltimore wrote on September 7, 1862, "I arrived here last evening from Washington, and had the pleasure of greeting another regiment of the brave sons of the 'Wooden Nutmeg State.'" "Nutmeg State" it was and would remain.

Did Connecticut peddlers really sell wooden replicas in place of real nutmegs to unsuspecting customers? No evidence has surfaced to date that such an exchange actually took place—nonetheless, human nature being what it is, it is not inconceivable that some unscrupulous Yankee might have tried to pull off such a scam.

One theory suggests that the wooden nutmeg story was a canard arising out of ignorance. Nutmegs are very hard and, when cracked, do not reveal edible meat as walnuts or butternuts do. Instead they break into fragments that do indeed look like pieces of wood. Someone not aware of that fundamental difference, who did not know that nutmegs were to be grated rather than cracked, might have concluded they had purchased a wooden fake.

In 1959 the General Assembly adopted the dignified, respectable "Constitution State" as Connecticut's official nickname. But more than half a century later, it shows no signs of eclipsing the older, spicier alternative: the "Nutmeg State."

BIBLIOGRAPHY

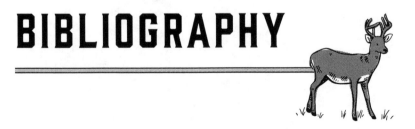

The First Witchcraft Executions in North America (1647–1663)

Demos, John Putnam. *Entertaining Satan: Witchcraft and the Culture of Early New England.* New York: Oxford University Press, 1982.

Marcus, Ronald. *"Elizabeth Clawson . . . Thou Deseruest to Dye": An Account of the Trial in 1692 of a Woman from Stamford, Connecticut, Who Was Accused of Being a Witch.* Stamford, CT: Stamford Historical Society, 1976.

Records of the Particular Court of Connecticut, 1639-1663. Connecticut Historical Society Collections. Vol. 22. Hartford: Connecticut Historical Society, 1928.

Ross, Richard S. III. *Witch Hunting in the Connecticut River Valley, 1647-1663.* Jefferson, NC: McFarland & Company, 2017.

Tomlinson, R. G. *Witchcraft Trials of Connecticut.* Hartford, CT: Bond Press, 1978.

Refugees from Royal Revenge (1660–1689)

Dexter, Franklin B. "Memoranda Respecting Edward Whalley and William Goffe." *Papers of the New Haven Colony Historical Society 2* (1877): 117–46.

Pagliuco, Christopher. *The Great Escape of Edward Whalley and William Goffe, Smuggled Through Connecticut.* Charleston, SC: History Press, 2012.

Trowbridge, Thomas R. "Remarks on Mr. Dexter's Paper Respecting Whalley and Goffe." *Papers of the New Haven Colony Historical Society 2* (1877): 147–53.

Welles, Lemuel A. *The History of the Regicides in New England.* New York: Grafton Press, 1927.

———. *The Regicides in Connecticut.* New Haven, CT: Yale University Press for the Tercentenary Commission of the State of Connecticut, 1935.

Hostile Takeover, Colonial Style (1665)

"Leete, William." American National Biography Online. https://anb .org.

"New Haven Colony." Wikipedia. https://en.wikipedia.org/wiki / New_Haven_Colony.

Public Records of the Colony of Connecticut prior to the Union with New Haven Colony, May, 1665. Hartford, CT: Brown and Parsons, 1850.

Israel Putnam, Original American Folk Hero (1718–1790)

Larned, Ellen. *History of Windham County, Connecticut, Volume 1, 1600 to 1760.* Worcester, MA: The Author, 1874.

Lockhart, Paul. *The Whites of Their Eyes: Bunker Hill, the First American Army, and the Emergence of George Washington.* New York: HarperCollins, 2011.

Niven, John. *Connecticut Hero: Israel Putnam.* Hartford: American Revolution Bicentennial Commission of Connecticut, 1977.

Newgate's Caverns for Criminals (1773–1827)

Phelps, Richard D. *Newgate of Connecticut: Its Origin and Early History. New and expanded edition.* Camden, ME: Pictou Press, 1996.

Springman, Mary Jane, and Betty Finnell Guinan. *East Granby: The Evolution of a Connecticut Town.* Canaan, NH: Phoenix Publishing for the East Granby Historical Committee, 1983.

Stealth *Turtle* (1775-1776)

Connecticut River Museum. ctrivermuseum.org/turtle-submarine.

Grant, Marion Hepburn. *The Infernal Machine of Saybrook's David Bushnell.* Old Saybrook, CT: Bicentennial Committee of Old Saybrook, 1976.

Lefkowitz, Arthur S. *Bushnell's Submarine: The Best Kept Secret of the American Revolution.* New York: Scholastic, 2006.

Submarine Force Library and Museum. https://ussnautilus.org/museum-information.

Swanson, June. *David Bushnell and His Turtle: The Story of America's First Submarine.* New York: Atheneum, 1991.

Melted Majesty (1776)

Bangs, Edward, ed. *Journal of Lieutenant Isaac Bangs: April 1 to July 29, 1776.* Cambridge: MA: John Wilson, 1890.

Bellion, Wendy. "A Toppled Statue of George III Illuminates the Ongoing Debate Over America's Monuments." *Smithsonian Magazine*, 28 January 2022.

Museum of the American Revolution. "'Melted Majesty' Musket Ball Discovered at Monmouth Battlefield to be Displayed at Museum for July 9 Anniversary." July 6, 2017.

Ruppert, Bob. "The Statue of George III." *Journal of the American Revolution*, September 8, 2014.

"Oliver Wolcott." The Society of the Descendants of the Signers of the Declaration of Independence. https://www.dsdi1776.com/oliver-wolcott.com.

Skinner Auctioneers. "Lead Hand, Wrist, and Forearm Likely from the Statue of King George III at Bowling Green, New York City." Historic Arms and Militaria Auction, November 4, 2019. skinnerinc.com.

Solly, Meilan. "You Could Own an Amputated Arm from the George III Statue Toppled at Bowling Green." *Smithsonian Magazine*, October 31, 2019. www.smithsonianmag.com.

The Dark Day (1780)

Connecticut Courant, May 23, 1780.

Connecticut Gazette, May 26, 1780.

Connecticut Journal, May 25, 1780.

Larned, Ellen D. *History of Windham County, Volume 2.* Worcester, MA: The Author, 1880.

Ludlum, David. *The Country Journal New England Weather Book.* Boston: Houghton-Mifflin, 1976.

———. "New England's Dark Day: 19 May 1780." *Weatherwise*, June 1972.

Public Records of the State of Connecticut, from May, 1780, to October, 1781. Hartford: Case, Lockwood & Brainard, 1922.

Seeley, Dorothy M. "Why Was Friday, May 19, 1780, a Dark Day in Connecticut?" Unpublished manuscript, 1983.

Massacre at Fort Griswold (1781)

Allyn, Charles. *The Battle of Groton Heights.* New London, CT: The Author, 1882.

Malley, Richard. *Blood on the Hill: The Battle of Groton Heights, September 6, 1781* — Connecticut History | a CTHumanities Project.

Powell, Walter Louis. "The New London Raid, 1781." Unpublished master's thesis, Kent State University, December 1978.

Smith, Carolyn, and Helen Vergason. *September 6, 1781: North Groton's Story.* New London, CT: New London Printers, 1981.

George Washington's Inauguration Suit (1789)

Author's email correspondence with Amanda Isaac, Associate Curator, George Washington's Mount Vernon, 25 March 2022.

Daily Advertiser, January 19, 1789.

Ford, Paul Leicester. *The True George Washington.* 10th edition. Philadelphia: J.B. Lippincott, 1896.

Grant, Ellsworth Strong. *Yankee Dreamers and Doers.* Chester, CT: Pequot Press, 1973.

New-York Packet, May 5, 1789.

Salem Mercury, March 31, 1789.

Walsh, James P. *Connecticut Industry and the Revolution.* Hartford, CT: American Revolution Bicentennial Commission of Connecticut, 1978.

Washington, George, to Daniel Hinsdale, April 8, 1789.

Washington, George, to Henry Knox, January 29, 1789.

The First American Cookbook (1796)

Brown, Martha C. "Of Pearl Ash, Emptins, and Tree Sweetnin'." *American Heritage* (May 1981). http://www.american heritage .com.

Simmons, Amelia. *American Cookery . . . A Facsimile of the Second Edition*, Printed in Albany, 1796, with an Introduction by Karen Hess. Bedford: Applewood Books, 1996.

Stavely, Keith, and Kathleen Fitzgerald. *United Tastes: The Making of the First American Cookbook.* Amherst: University of Massachusetts Press, 2017.

Perkins's Tractors (1796–1810)

Quen, Jacques Marc. "A Study of Dr. Elisha Perkins and Perkinism." Unpublished thesis, Yale University, 1954.

Steiner, Walter R. *Dr. Elisha Perkins of Plainfield, Conn., and His Metallic Tractors.* Hartford, CT: Reprinted from the Bulletin of the Society of Medical History of Chicago [1923].

Young, James Harvey. *The Toadstool Millionaires: A Social History of Patent Medicines in America before Federal Regulations.* Princeton, NJ: Princeton University Press, 1961.

Good for Whatever Ails Ya (1796–1850)

Connecticut Courant, August 10, 1835.

Connecticut Medical Society *Proceedings of the President and Fellows . . . at Their Annual Convention in New Haven, October 16 and 17, 1805.*

Eastern Argus [Portland, ME], September 4, 1829.

Massachusetts Mercury, May 12, 1797; June 4, 1799.

Norwich Courier, July 26, 1798; August 16 and 23, 1798; August 10, 1831.

Providence Gazette, September 24, 1796.

Salem Register, August 19, 1802.

Young, James Harvey. *The Medical Messiahs: A Social History of Health Quackery in Twentieth-Century America*. Princeton, NJ: Princeton University Press, 1966.

———. *The Toadstool Millionaires: A Social History of Patent Medicines in America before Federal Regulations*. Princeton, NJ: Princeton University Press, 1961.

Turning 'Em Out like Clockwork (1814)

"Eli Terry." Wikipedia. https://en.wikipedia.org/wiki/Eli_Terry.

Grant, Ellsworth Strong. *Yankee Dreamers and Doers*. Chester, CT: Pequot Press, 1973.

Jerome, Chauncey. *History of the American Clock Business for the Past Sixty Years*. New Haven, CT: F.C. Dayton, 1860.

Breaking the Soundless Barrier (1817)

American Asylum, at Hartford, for the Education and Instruction of the Deaf and Dumb. *A Brief History of the American Asylum, at Hartford, for the Education and Instruction of the Deaf and Dumb*. Hartford, CT: Case, Lockwood & Brainard, 1893.

"American School for the Deaf." Wikipedia. https://en.wikipedia.org/wiki/American_School_for_the_Deaf.

"Brief History of ASD." American School for the Deaf. https://www.asd-1817.org/about/history--cogswell-heritage-house.

"Hartford Area Sites Important to the History of Deaf Education."
West Hartford, CT: American School for the Deaf, n.d.

"Gallaudet University. The Legacy Begins." https://www.gallaudet
.edu/about/history-and-traditions/the-legacy-begins.

Burning Rubber (1839)

"Charles Goodyear." *Scientific American Supplement,* January 31,
1891.

"Charles Goodyear." Wikipedia. https://en.wikipedia.org/wiki/
Charles_Goodyear.

Korman, Richard. *The Goodyear Story: An Inventor's Obsession and
the Struggle for a Rubber Monopoly.* San Francisco: Encounter
Books, 2002.

Slack, Charles. *Noble Obsession: Charles Goodyear, Thomas
Hancock, and the Race to Unlock the Greatest Industrial Secret of
the Nineteenth Century.* New York: Hyperion, 2002.

"Vulcanization." Wikipedia. https://en.wikipedia.org/wiki /
Vulcanized_rubber.

Pain Killer (1844)

Hartford Daily Courant, December 9, 1846; January 25, 1848.

———. "The Late Horace Wells," "Horace Wells," January 26,
1848.

Cedar Hill Cemetery & Foundation, Hartford, CT. https://www
.cedarhillcemetery.org/notable-resident/dr-horace-wells/

Wright, A. J. "Horace Wells, D.D.S.: Rebel with a Cause."
Newsletter, American Society of Anesthesiologists, September
1999.

A Connecticut Yankee on Baker Street, William Gillette (1853-1937)

Barnes, Alan. *Sherlock Holmes on Screen: The Complete Film and
TV History.* London: Titan Books, 2011.

de Castella, Tom. "William Gillette: Five ways he transformed how Sherlock Holmes looks and talks." *BBC News Magazine.* January 26, 2015. https://www.bbc.com/news/magazine-30932322.

Gillette Castle State Park, Wikipedia, https://en.wikipedia.org/wiki/ Gillette_Castle_State_Park.

Higham, Charles. *The Adventures of Conan Doyle.* New York: W.W. Norton, 1976.

Zecher, Henry. *William Gillette, America's Sherlock Holmes.* Xlibris Corporation, 2011.

Abby Smith and Her Cows (1873-1878)

Housley, Kathleen L. *The Letter Kills but the Spirit Gives Life: The Smiths—Abolitionists, Suffragists, Bible Translators.* Glastonbury, CT: Historical Society of Glastonbury, 1993.

Smith, Julia E. *Abby Smith and Her Cows with a Report of the Law Case Decided Contrary to Law.* Hartford; The Author, 1877.

The Father of American Football (1880s)

Breglio, Nola. "Camp's Legacy Lives on in the Game." *Yale Herald,* November 19, 1998.

"Camp and His Followers: American Football, 1876–1889." Professional Football Researchers Association. http://footballresearch .com/articles/frpage_topic_d-to1889.html.

"History of American Football." Wikipedia. https://en.wikipedia .org /wiki/History_of_American_football.

"Walter Camp, 1859–1925." http://www.waltercamp.org /history5 .htm.

"Walter Camp." Wikipedia. https://en.wikipedia.org/wiki /Walter_ Camp.

The Great Blizzard (1888)

Caplovich, Judd. *Blizzard! The Great Storm of '88.* Vernon, CT: VeRo Publishing, 1987.

Hartford Courant, March 13, 14, 16, 17, 23, 1888.

New York Times, March 18, 1888.

Arsenic and Multiple Homicide (1910-1919)

Hartford Courant, "Alienists Declare Mrs. Gilligan Insane," June 27, 1919.

———. "Amy E. Archer Gilligan Found Guilty of First Degree Murder; Sentenced to Be Hanged Nov. 6," July 14, 1917.

———. "Cumulative Evidence Offered by Prosecution in Gilligan Murder Case," July 4, 1917.

———. "Enough Arsenic Found in Andrews's Stomach to Kill Several Men," June 27, 1917.

———. "Exhume Body of Gilligan, Second Husband of Archer Woman, for Poison Evidence," July 2, 1916.

———. "Gilligan Trial Alienists Go into Secret Conference," June 20, 1919.

———. "Mrs. Gilligan Is Indicted on Five Counts of Murder," September 22, 1916.

———. "Mrs. Gilligan Pleads Guilty in Second Degree; Sent to Prison for Life," July 2, 1919.

———. "New Trial for Mrs. Gilligan," May 1, 1918.

———. "Poison Expert Testifies Acute Arsenic Poisoning Caused Death of Andrews," June 19, 1919.

———. "Police Believe Archer Home for Aged a Murder Factory"; "Mrs. Gilligan on the Grill"; "Vituperative Letters Written by Mrs. Gilligan—Extortion of Money"; and "Brief Life Story of Mrs. Gilligan," May 9, 1916.

———. "State's Attorney Concludes Argument in Gilligan Case: Judge to Charge Jury Today," July 13, 1917.

———. "To Charge 5 Murders in Asking Indictment of Archer Home Woman," September 13, 1916.

Owens, David. "Windsor Woman Poisoned Multiple Tenants of Her Home for the Elderly." *Hartford Courant*, April 17, 2014.

Phelps, M. William. "Amy Archer Gilligan: Entrepreneur, Caretaker, Serial Killer." Amazon Shorts, 2006.

A Lady Governor, but Never a Governor's First Lady (1975)

Bysiewicz, Susan. *Ella: A Biography of Governor Ella Grasso*. Old Saybrook, CT: Peregrine Press, 1984.

"Ella Giovanna Oliva (Tambussi) Grasso, Governor of Connecticut, 1975–1980." https://museumofcthistory.org/2015/08/ella -giovanna-oliva-tambussi-grasso/.

Hamilton, Robert A. "Capitol Getting a Statue of Grasso." *Hartford Courant*, February 1, 1987.

Martin, Antoinette. "She Never Considered Being a Woman a Political Liability." *Hartford Courant*, February 6, 1981.

Purmont, Jon E. "The Education of Ella Grasso." *Hog River Journal*, August/September/October 2004.

Raynor, Vivian. "Contemporary Approach to an Age-Old Tradition." *Hartford Courant*, February 1, 1987.

Miraculous Disaster (1978)

Baugus, R. V. "Frankly Speaking." Facility Manager, International Association of Assembly Managers, June–July 2006. "Hartford Settles Roof-Collapse Suit." *New York Times*, March 28, 1984.

Victor, Omotoriogun. "The Hartford Civic Centre roof collapse." Structures Centre. May 25, 2020. https://structurescentre.com/ the-hartford-civic-centre-roof-collapse/

"It Was 25 Years Ago Today." *Hartford Courant*, January 18, 2003.

Martin, Rachel. "Hartford Civic Center Arena Roof Collapse" report prepared for 1999 Research Experiences for Undergraduates Site sponsored by University of Alabama at Birmingham Department of Civil and Environmental Engineering.

"The Night the Roof Fell In." *Time*, January 30, 1978.

Hangin' with the Governor (1991)

Connecticut Courant, September 2, 1765.

Johnson, Kirk. "Lawmakers Tell 40,000 at Rally Connecticut Income Tax Will Die." *New York Times*, October 6, 1991.

New London Gazette, August 23 and 30, 1765; November 8, 1765.

New York Times, "Remnants for a Museum," October 9, 1991.

Weicker, Lowell P., Jr., with Barry Sussman. *Maverick: A Life in Politics*. Boston: Little, Brown, 1995.

Remembering 9/11 (2002–Today)

Clapper, Rob. "The Making of a Memorial." *Landscape Architecture News Digest*, American Association of Landscape Architects, September 15, 2003. http://www.asla.org.

Condon, Garret. "State's Hospitals Prepare for Worst." *Hartford Courant*, September 12, 2001.

"Connecticut's 9-11 Living Memorial." Sherwood Island State Park—CTs 9-11 Living Memorial. https://portal.ct.gov/DEEP/ State-Parks/Parks/Sherwood-Island-State-Park/CTs-9-11-Living-Memorial.

"Connecticut's 9-11 Living Memorial." Living Memorials Project National Registry. http://www.livingmemorialsproject.net / registry.

Spears, Natalie. "An Evolving Tribute: Connecticut's 9/11 Memorial." Dust Settled, *Medium*. https://medium.com/ dust-settled/an-evolving-tribute-connecticuts-9-11-memorial-3c20b2ade40c.

Moreau, Carolyn. "State Wants to Help Day After Disaster." *Hartford Courant*, September 13, 2001.

The 9-11 Living Memorial at Sherwood Island State Park in Westport, Connecticut's Oldest State Park. https://www .thedistractedwanderer.com/2012/01/9-11-living-memorial-at -sherwood-island.html.

Salzman, Avi. "Recalling September 11, Quietly." *New York Times*, September 11, 2005.

The Nutmeg State (1800s–Today)

Baltimore Patriot, June 27, 1818; July 17, 1823.

Bartlett, John Russell. *Dictionary of Americanisms*. 1859.

Goodrich, Samuel Griswold. *Recollections of a Lifetime, Volume I.* New York: Miller, Orton and Mulligan, 1856.

Hartford Daily Courant, April 30, 1861; September 16, 1862.

Hill, D. H. *Elements of Hill's Algebra*. Philadelphia: J. B. Lippincott & Co., 1857.

Rainer, Joseph. "The 'Sharper' Image: Yankee Peddlers, Southern Consumers, and the Market Revolution." *Business and Economic History* 26, no. 1 (Fall 1997).

Vermont Intelligencer, March 31, 1817.

INDEX

ACKNOWLEDGMENTS

Like every historian, I am indebted to a chain of individuals, some known, others anonymous. They include the people who made the history, those who created some record of it at the time it occurred, those who deliberately or inadvertently held onto those records for decades or even centuries, those who have collected and preserved these records and made them available for research, and in many cases historians both amateur and professional whose writings provide authors undertaking their own exploration of a topic with invaluable facts, context, and interpretation. In the specific case of *It Happened in Connecticut*, I must thank my original editor at Globe Pequot Press, Amy Paradysz. It was Amy who initially got me involved in this project, and her support, encouragement, and assistance made fulfilling it a pleasure.

ABOUT THE AUTHOR

Diana Ross McCain has written about Connecticut's past for more than thirty-five years. She holds bachelor's and master's degrees in history, and a master's degree in library science. She was on the staff of the Connecticut Historical Society for twenty-five years. A frequent contributor to *Early American Life* and *Connecticut* magazines and other publications, McCain wrote the award-winning publication *To All on Equal Terms*, the story of Connecticut's official state heroine, Prudence Crandall. She is the author of *Thy Children's Children: A Historical Novel Based on the True Story of Five Generations of a New England Grassroots Dynasty*, the Lyman family of Middlefield, Connecticut's, Lyman Orchards. She lives in Durham, Connecticut.